The Guerrilla Guide to Animation

The Guerrilla Guide to Animation

MAKING ANIMATED FILMS OUTSIDE THE MAINSTREAM

Walter Santucci

continuum

NEW YORK • LONDON

2009

The Continuum International Publishing Group Inc
80 Maiden Lane, New York, NY 10038

The Continuum International Publishing Group Ltd
The Tower Building, 11 York Road, London SE1 7NX

www.continuumbooks.com

Library of Congress Cataloging-in-Publication Data
Santucci, Walter.
  The guerrilla guide to animation : making animated films outside the mainstream / by Walter Santucci.
      p. cm.
  Includes bibliographical references.
  ISBN-13: 978-0-8264-2985-8 (pbk. : alk. paper)
  ISBN-10: 0-8264-2985-8 (pbk. : alk. paper) 1. Animated films—Technique. 2. Animation (Cinematography) I. Title.

  NC1765.S26 2009
  791.43'34—dc22

                                        2008046009

Printed in the United States of America

ISBN 9780826429407

Acknowledgments

I would like to thank David Barker and the Continuum International Publishing Group for making this book possible. I would also like to thank Grace Park for her invaluable help in digitizing and adjusting the many illustrations.

Contents

PART II: ANECDOTAL SECTION

PART I

Preface

An Unlikely Journey into Animation

As a kid, I did not draw and I had absolutely no inclination to do so. Art class in school was *boring*. (Actually, *all* of school was boring.) But I always loved animation.

I did not go to animation school. Yet, less than a month after graduating from film school, I sold an animated movie to Cinemax. Though funny, it was crudely animated and my classmates thought I was stupid to try and sell it. But I went ahead regardless.

Without knowing what I was doing (at first), I managed over the next twenty years to build myself a successful animation career. And that's why I am writing *Guerrilla Animation: A Guide to Making Animated Films Outside the Mainstream*—to show the way for outsiders who want to succeed in the industry or who merely want to make good films on their own.

Guerrilla Animation is divided into two sections. Part One is an instructional section, which teaches animation basics along with short-cuts and cheats. Part Two is an anecdotal section, the content of which is culled from my twenty years of experience in the world of animation. The main thrust of both sections is to show non-traditional ways to create professional-looking animation. I will teach the rules, but I will also show how, when, and why to break them.

Right now there are tens of thousands of people around the world making crappy little animated films* and posting them on YouTube. It is human nature that many of them will want to improve their skills as they make more films. This book will show them how.

---

* I am not passing judgement. I started out making crappy little films and soon found myself wanting to improve my skills. Crappy little films are awesome.

Introduction to
the Entire Book

Why does this book exist? I mean, beyond the fact that I typed it into a computer and hit SAVE when I was done?

It is to provide the outsider, the anarchist, the rebel, the GUERRILLA, guidance into the world of 2D animation. It is to provide the tools and knowledge needed to make animated films to those who can't afford animation training, or who seek to find an alternate path.

It will also work on normal people.

"What is 2D animation?" some of you may be asking. "2D" refers mainly to traditional, hand-drawn animation (like Bugs Bunny or *Family Guy*) but can also include other styles such as "cut-out" animation (like in *Monty Python's Flying Circus**).

What this book does *not* deal with is 3D computer-generated animation, that is, animation that utilizes such software as Maya.

You see, computer-generated 3D animation is a whole other ball of worms. But if you learn what's in this book, you can be a good 3D animator, because the essentials of timing and rhythm apply to both genres.

DO YOU HAVE TO KNOW HOW TO DRAW OR BE GOOD AT DRAWING?

Drawing ability was the last thing I thought of when I began animating (look at this still from my first film if you don't believe me):

While most 2D animation is created with drawings, I figured being *funny* was more important. Yes, I eventually taught myself to draw, but

---

* What about *South Park*? Isn't that cut-out animation? Well, the original pilot, "Spirit of Christmas," was, but now the show is actually made using 3D software.

I also made (and sold) films while learning. In fact, any animator will tell you that you *never* stop learning to draw.

So, the answer to the above question is no. If your ideas are good, you can still make good animation without knowing how to draw. Look at *South Park*. The artwork on that show is not impressive in any technical or aesthetic sense. But the show is usually funny and well written.

Now look at *Anastasia*. Lots of highly skilled artists worked on that film, but it came out looking like doo-doo on a stick. Why? No inspiration. Too much corporate involvement. Too many internal committees. Too many producers thinking more about their BMWs than about doing a good job.

So, as long as you don't think only about luxury cars, you won't have to know how to draw. Until you want to.

Introduction to
the Instructional Section

If you are going to animate, you are going to need *something* to do it with. This book explains methods for using pencil and paper as well as today's commonly used software packages such as Flash, After Effects, and Photoshop. Not everybody will have access to all these things, but the most important skill for a rebel animator is the ability to improvise and make whatever you *do* have work.

For example, if you have a pen and a pad of Post-it notes, you can draw pictures on every Post-it, each slightly different from the other:

If you do this, you will have created a flipbook.* You will have created animation.

Of course, your pad of Post-it notes will be difficult to put on television unless you scan every page into a computer and output it into a viewable format.

Luckily, more important to animation than technology is a GOOD IDEA. These you can create for *free*. The only thing better than a good idea is a *great* idea. These you can also create for free, or I can sell you one for $75.

If you have good ideas, then turning them into finished films is merely a rewarding journey you can and will make if you have the desire.

This book will help you along the path.

---

*A flipbook, in case you didn't know, is a series of animation drawings bound into a small book, which when flipped via your thumb, plays back a little movie. Come on, I *know* you know what I'm talking about. Don't be that way! In fact, there are several flipbooks in the margins of this very book—so start flipping!

And by the way, you probably won't agree with my opinions about many things in this book. For example, I think Steven Spielberg is a mediocre filmmaker whose ideas are obvious, whose manipulations are obtuse, and whose scripts serve no real purpose. I think Jim Carrey is tiresome, annoying, and has no idea what funny is. You, however, like most people, might think both these fine gentlemen are geniuses. This will in no way diminish the lessons in this book. Merely smirk and shake your head in pity when I offer such opinions. However, when I say that 24 frames per second is a hugely important concept to grasp, you'd better *listen*, dammit, because that is not opinion, that is the TRUTH!

CHAPTER 1

What Is Animation?

Here is a dry, succinct definition of animation that sounds like it came from the *New World Collegiate Dictionary and Style Guide*, but which I actually made up just now: "Animation is a moving picture created via photographing or digitizing inanimate objects or drawings in succession."

Hand-drawn animation is a series of drawings, each slightly different, which, when viewed in succession, seem to move.

Let me illustrate. On this page and the next odd-numbered page are two pictures of the same characters. But they are in very different positions in each picture.

Flip back and forth between the two pages and you will see very basic animation. These drawings are known as EXTREME poses. They are key moments of an action.

I might want the action to be this stark, but more likely I will want to put some drawings in between them.

The technical term for a drawing between extreme poses is an INBETWEEN. I have made one inbetween in this instance. Flip pages 13, 15, and 17, and look at how the inbetween fills in the action.

When animating, the number of inbetweens depends on the desired look or effect the artist envisions. For example, if I wanted the scene in slow motion, I would do many more inbetweens. But more on that later. Well, if you want more *now*, flip the upper corner of the book—the part with these same characters in the same scene. You'll see a fully fleshed out animation with anticipation, reaction, follow-through, and other neat junk you'll learn a little later.

Of course, you might not want to draw your animation. You might want to manipulate cut-outs or clay figures under the camera, which is fine—but you will still follow many of the same rules for hand-drawn, which is the main focus of this book.

CHAPTER 2

Materials

While there are many types of software out there to help do the grunt work of animation, it's best to know how traditional animation is created before using them.

For your work, the first thing you will need is what is called a "peg bar." The second thing you will need is also called a "peg bar." Because you will need two peg bars.

"But," you might be saying, "I have neither of these things and even if I did, I wouldn't know it because I have no idea what you are talking about."

Well then.

See this picture on the right?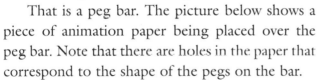

That is a peg bar. The picture below shows a piece of animation paper being placed over the peg bar. Note that there are holes in the paper that correspond to the shape of the pegs on the bar.

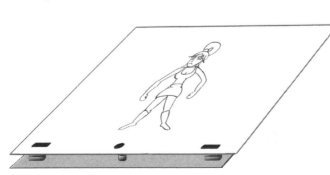

The peg bar's purpose is to keep your drawings from moving while you work, holding them in place while you create the many pictures needed to make your artwork come alive.

If you're unfamiliar with the technical side of animation, then the pegs on the peg bar will look unusual to you. They are called "acme" pegs, and that's the basic configuration of pegs in most animation studios. So if you order animation paper that has the holes prepunched, you order "acme punched" paper. Unlike the Acme products ordered by Wile E. Coyote, this paper is rarely defective.

It is possible, by the way, to get an animation peg bar with pegs that fit ordinary three-hole-punched paper. Lightfoot, Inc. (see Appendix) makes these, and as an independent animator you might want to choose this style since regular copier paper is cheaper than animation paper and you can punch it yourself with a three-hole punch.

Just be forewarned that regular hole punchers are not as precise as professional animation punchers, so your work might be slightly less accurate. Another reason to use acme-punched paper is that if you are working back and forth with other animators who are set up traditionally, you won't be able to swap drawings because you'll be using different types of peg bars.

Regardless of the type, using a peg bar is the basic way to keep animation drawings "registered" with one another, bringing order to the chaos you so badly want to create. Yes, there are times when we need order, and this is one of them.

Why *two* peg bars? Because you will need one for your SCANNER and one for your LIGHT BOX.

What is a scanner? I'm talking about the piece of hardware connected to a computer which allows you to digitize artwork. It will be very helpful for you to have one of these, with a peg bar taped to the edge (see illustration), on which you will place your animation. Once taped onto your scanner, this peg bar should be removed only in dire circumstances. If you never move it, five years from now you can insert a new drawing into the animation you create today and it will fit right in.

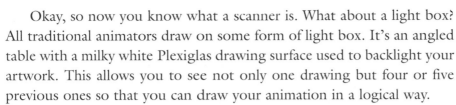

Okay, so now you know what a scanner is. What about a light box? All traditional animators draw on some form of light box. It's an angled table with a milky white Plexiglas drawing surface used to backlight your artwork. This allows you to see not only one drawing but four or five previous ones so that you can draw your animation in a logical way.

You can buy a very expensive, really awesome light-box desk for between $500 and $1000, or a portable, personal one for between $70 and $120. Or you can build one for about $30 or less.

A very expensive animation desk with free kitten.

And here's how:

1. Buy a piece of lumber (scrap pine will do) that is approximately 15" wide, 1" thick, and 10–12" deep.

2. Buy a pair of metal shelving brackets about 7" long (and screws to fit).

EITHER

3. Buy a piece of milky white Plexiglas at least 12" by 12" square (usually about $10–15; see Appendix for sources), along with a peg bar.

OR

4. Buy a prefabricated Plexiglas inking board from an animation supply house (about $30; see Appendix for suppliers) with a built-in peg bar.

5. Buy a piece of thin wood the same length as the lumber from #1: 1.5" tall, maybe 1/4" thick.

6. Screw the brackets to the board as far apart as you can and still being able to rest the Plexiglas on it. Put duct tape on the tips of the brackets so they don't scratch your Plexiglas.

7. Nail the thin piece of wood to the front of the board as a lip to keep the Plexiglas from sliding off.

8. Buy a small reading lamp.

9. Place said lamp on its side behind the Plexiglas.

10. If your peg bar is still lying around, tape it to the bottom of the Plexiglas.

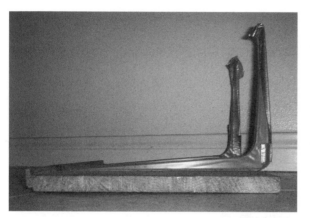

And boo-yaa! You have a light box! I've animated many professional jobs on a total Fred Sanford rig like this, and so can you.

Other things you will need:

1. Animation paper. This comes in many varieties. For a beginner on a budget I would suggest punched 10 field student bond paper. (See the Appendix for suppliers.)

What does all that mean? Most studios use what is called 12 field paper. 10 field paper is the same size as letter-sized copier paper. 12 field is a little bigger. It's also more expensive (by at least $10 per 500 sheets), and since 10 field is perfectly cromulent to animate with, why not save some money? Besides, many Japanese studios use 10 field paper, and most Japanese studios are totally wicked cool. Maybe it's the paper.

It is best to buy prepunched paper. To punch it yourself you'll have to buy a special animation puncher and these cost about $1,000. It's not like a regular three-hole punch. It's a precision machine.

If you have access to a puncher (meaning you or someone you know works at an animation studio), then you can buy reams of regular letter-sized paper, punch it, and go on with your bad self.

2. Pencils. Most animators use erasable blue pencils for their rough work. Not everyone uses them, but I do and this is my book. A company called Col-Erase makes them. They are getting harder to find at local art stores but can be ordered in bulk on the web. I get best results by doing an online search for "col-erase blue pencils cheap."

   You'll also want black pencils, but not typical school pencils. Try some out at an art store and find a brand you are comfortable with. Then, once more, go on with your bad self.

3. A kneaded eraser. Not essential, but I find it a useful way to erase my crappy lines, leaving only the essentials.

4. A good eraser.

5. OR, if you decide to eschew paper and pencil and work exclusively in Flash, you will need Flash and a drawing tablet. You *could* try drawing with a mouse, but don't say I didn't warn you.

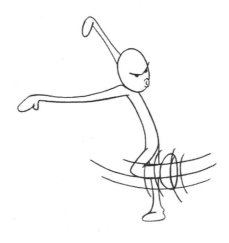

CHAPTER 3

Basic Computer Knowledge

This book assumes basic computer literacy on the part of the reader. You should know how to turn your computer on, how to save projects, where to save them, and what it means to "click" on something.

You shouldn't panic, grab a broom, and smash things when someone tells you there is a mouse next to your computer. You should be familiar with menu bars, tool boxes, arrows, and methods of deleting, and you should know that the retractable cup holder is in actuality a DVD drive.

Try to be a "cross platform" person, i.e., be comfortable on both Macs and PCs. I started out on a Mac, but for animation I have had to become PC oriented. Why? Most software essential to 2D animation only exists for PCs, though this situation is changing. Instructions in this book assume the user is on a PC. If you are using a Mac and your mouse can't right click, use CTRL click instead. Also, Mac users take note that any instruction, except the previous one, where I say to use the CTRL key, you use the command (or "apple") key.

CHAPTER 4

What Is an Adequate Computer Setup?

In order to use Flash and After Effects, an animator needs a computer with proper amounts of memory, enough RAM, a good graphics card, etc. This chapter covers minimum and optimum requirements. You should get as much RAM and memory as you can afford, as well as the best graphics card you can.

What does all that mean? RAM (random access memory) is the temporary memory your computer uses to run programs. It is the memory used while you work. The more you have, the faster and smoother your software will run.

"Memory" refers to the secondary memory system in your computer. Whatever is in your RAM goes away when you turn your computer off, so there's a secondary memory in the computer for long-term storage. When doing animation, you will want to store a lot of data on your computer, so get as much memory as you can afford.

A graphics card (or video card) is a piece of hardware in your computer that generates and outputs images. You should get the most powerful and advanced one you can find.

Here's a little list of what a good computer setup should have:

- CPU with two DVD burner drives, one gig of RAM, 100 gigs of storage

- Two monitors
- Two external firewire or USB drives
- A top-notch graphics card

BUT, you can get away with one DVD burner drive, one monitor, and one external drive, and instead of using a top-notch graphics card you can use a gaming card, which is cheaper but still good. That's what I do.

Also, get a website so you can display your work and make it accessible to the world. The ftp site which will come with your website allows you to post your work for clients and colleagues as well. This ftp site is also a nice backup place to store your important work.

A NOTE ON SOFTWARE

Software will change. Rapidly. Every few years you will have to learn how to use the new piece of "hot" software (not hot meaning stolen; hot meaning it is, like, totally popular), and even the older software keeps evolving so you will have to learn new features. Next year's versions of Flash and After Effects will undoubtedly have something new and cool on them.

But if you know the basics of traditional animation, you can adapt to whatever new thing comes along. For the time being, I will give you some essentials in Flash, FlipBook, and After Effects. But that's a couple of chapters away. Before that you need to learn ANIMATION.

CHAPTER 5

Animation Basics

24 FRAMES PER SECOND (FPS)

In one second of film, there are 24 frames.

For every second you watch at a movie theater, 24 separate pictures flash on the screen. Therefore, in animation, you might have to draw 24 pictures for every second—you can usually get away with 12, showing each for two frames, but the point to learn is:

EVERY SECOND THAT GOES BY
CONTAINS 24 FRAMES.

Is this really important? *Yes.* It's the most important lesson to learn in the world of animation. It applies to *South Park*, it applies to *Family Guy*, it applies to *Fantasia*, and it applies to *The Incredibles*. Every other aspect of timing and pacing come from understanding this. You must get a feel for it.

For example, if you are working on a scene and you want a character to look skeptical "for a second," do you really mean one second, that is, 24 frames? Or would a second and a half (32 frames) look better?

The greater your feel for 24 frames per second, the quicker you will be able to make such timing decisions. How do you get a good grasp of this concept?

These six frames are merely one quarter of a second of film time.

Try the following exercise. It will allow you to see how many frames something needs to be on screen to be noticed. A good general rule is that six frames is the minimum, but through experimenting you will come up with your own numbers and theories.

To do this exercise you will need Flash or DigiCel FlipBook or Photoshop Extended to play it back.

"What?" you might be thinking. "I don't have that software. I spent my lunch money on this stupid book, I can't afford some stupid computer program too!"

Hey, relax. This is Cool Walt you're talking to. I'll hook you up. It just so happens that you can get these programs FREE from the web. And from the manufacturers, *with their full knowledge and consent*!

They will only be trial versions, and as such have some limitations, but you will be able to use them and decide whether you might want to eventually buy them.

Flash's trial version is absolutely complete, but you only have 30 days to use it. BUT 30 days is long enough to learn it. When I first learned Flash for a job, I used the free version and was good to go in just over two weeks.

Photoshop, like Flash, is an Adobe product, and it too is available for a free 30-day trial. Photoshop is a great animation tool. It allows an artist to make fantastic backgrounds and other elements in a short amount of time. In late 2007, for example, while writing this very book, I made a theatrical commercial for the TV show *Lost*. I had to recreate the look and feel of a classic movie theater ad, including singing refreshments encouraging patrons to go to the lobby. Using Photoshop (and its tools and filters), I was able to create, in a few hours, a background for the theater interior that looked as if I had spent days painting it.

DigiCel FlipBook's trial version can be used *forever*. BUT everything you make with it will have a DIGICEL FLIPBOOK watermark printed over it, making it impossible to output something commercially. Still, you can do some exercises this way (the GUERRILLA way, dammit!), and if you like the software (I give it two thumbs up), it is *very* inexpensive.

THE EXERCISE

The exercise is quite simple: CREATE A FIVE-SECOND ANIMA-TION, frame by frame, drawing by drawing, for 120 frames (five seconds). Do not double-expose drawings. Each frame must be an entirely new drawing.

You can do simple things like bouncing balls, you can write your name, make a dog drive a tank—whatever you want, as long as by the end you have drawn 120 frames.

If you want to draw on paper, get your light box out, take 120 sheets of paper and proceed. When you're done, scan each drawing into FlipBook or Photoshop and play them back.

Here's how to play back in Photoshop CS3 Extended:

1. Scan your drawings.

2. Save your scans and NUMBER THEM SEQUENTIALLY. Since you will have 120 drawings, the first should be numbered "001" and not "1" so the computer will see your sequence as the sequence it truly is.

3. Open Photoshop Extended.

4. Under FILE in the menu bar, chose OPEN.

5. A window will appear in which you can choose what to open. Find your sequence of drawings and select the first. At the bottom of the window will be a box next to the words IMAGE SEQUENCE. Check this box then click the OPEN button.

6. A window will open asking what frame rate you want. Type in "24" then hit "OK."

7. On the menu bar, click on WINDOW, then choose ANIMA-TION from the dropdown menu. This will give you your animation controls.

8. Click the PLAY button (the big arrow) and watch your animation. The first time it plays will be choppy because it's loading, but after that it will play smoothly.

With FlipBook, you can import your drawings with either a scanner or a camera. For simple testing I recommend a camera—it works much faster.

Continued

1. Open Flipbook.

2. Chose CREATE NEW SCENE.

3. On the menu bar, click the icon that looks like a camera on a stand. (Actually, I think it looks like a toothbrush.)

4. Click OK on the next two windows that pop up, after making sure the frame rate is 24 fps and the exposure rate is one.

5. Now you are ready to shoot. Press the space bar each time you wish to shoot a frame.

6. Having shot all your frames, click EXIT in the window at the bottom.

7. In the window that remains open on the screen, hit the PLAY button (the green arrow) and watch.

If you want to bypass paper and draw right into the computer, you can use Flash. In this instance, since your animation will probably be simple, you can get away with drawing with the mouse if you don't have a drawing tablet. Skip ahead to the Flash chapter, get familiar with the basics of the program, then do the following:

1. Open a new Flash document (set at 24 fps)

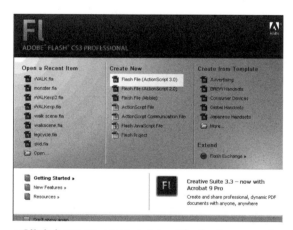

Click here to open a new Flash document.

2. In the timeline, select 120 frames and convert them to blank keyframes by pressing F6 once you've selected them.

Continued

3. Activate Onion Skin.

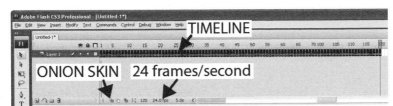

Here's the Flash timeline with 120 frames converted to keyframes.
The spots to change frame rate and activate Onion Skin are indicated.

4. Animate from frame 1 until you get to 120.

5. To play back, hit ENTER.

LAYERS

As the art of making animated films developed, animators quickly invented shortcuts and time-saving devices. By 1915, cels were invented. Cels saved enormous amounts of work and solved many problems. Unfortunately, cels themselves required an enormous amount of work and caused many problems, but until the digital age, they were the 2D animation standard.

So, what the hell are cels anyway, you ask? Cels are thin sheets of transparent plastic, the same size as animation paper, onto which animation drawings are inked or Xeroxed, then painted.

After they are painted, the painted area is opaque but the rest is clear, so, when placed over a background, the background is visible.

A character painted on a cel, over a background.

Why were cels so remarkable? Before their invention, animators either traced backgrounds over and over onto the character drawings (animation pioneer Winsor McCay's assistant John Fitzsimmons traced tens of thousands of backgrounds for McCay's films) or tore the paper around the characters and placed them over backgrounds, or didn't use backgrounds.

With cels, animators could not only have a separate background layer, but they could save time by separating a character's moving and non-moving parts onto different cel levels.

But *you* don't even have to deal with cels—you can break your animation up into layers DIGITALLY.

What this means, though, is you should start thinking in terms of layers when you plan your animation. It is often best to draw all the characters from a scene on separate sheets of paper, then stage them together on the computer.

In the illustration below, you see another use of layers: foregrounds. The fence goes in front of the character so you don't need to worry about conforming the character to the fence's contours:

Animation without foreground element.

Animation with foreground element.

ROUGHS, CLEANUPS, SCANNED, PAINTED

Your drawings might exist in up to four incarnations. The very first is ROUGH drawings. These are the first drawings you do. It is perfectly fine for these to be your final drawings as well, if you like a rough-and-dirty style.

By the way, I usually do my roughs with erasable blue pencil. Why? Because the lines are lighter than black pencil and I can work out my ideas very sketchily before committing myself. See all the circles in the rough drawing on the next page? Though this is a black-and-white picture, trust me, I did it with blue pencil:

If you want things neater, you can clean your drawings up. There are two ways to do this. The way I do it is born from having no budget for much of my career. Though the *professional* way to do a cleanup requires a fresh sheet of paper, I often did not have that luxury. So, I'd use a kneaded eraser and try to get rid of most of the dirt and grime on the rough, then I'd go over the remaining lines, making them sharp and clear. These are clean, in a way. I call them "nasty" cleanups. But the method has served me well. Here's a nasty cleanup:

When I clean up, I usually use black pencil, which will show up strong over the blue sketch lines. Here's another reason blue pencil makes sense for rough drawings: when you clean up the blue roughs with black, very few of the blue lines (especially since they've been semi-erased) will show up when you scan your drawings, which will be your next step.

Here's an example of a proper cleanup:

To do a proper cleanup, you put your rough on your light table upside down, then trace it lightly with blue or red on a new sheet. Remove the rough, flip the new drawing over so the clean side faces you and place that on the light table. You can see the colored pencil line even though it's on the other side of the paper. On the clean side, trace the colored line in black and the result will be a very clean drawing.

But you can forget most of that, because clean drawings are generally a waste of time to the guerrilla animator. Dirty is good!

Clean or not, your next step is to scan the drawings into whatever program you're using, wherein you shall also paint them. Here's a scanned and painted drawing:

Sweet!

INBETWEENS

In Chapter One, I mentioned inbetweens, which are the drawings inbetween extreme poses in animation. Your animation might not have inbetweens. If you animate "straight ahead," that is, draw frame by frame the way you did in the first exercise, you won't add inbetweens (unless, of course, you want to make timing changes).

However, it is often easier to animate "pose to pose," that is, draw the extremes of the action first, then add inbetweens.

One thing about using inbetweens is if you make your extreme drawings really nice, you can fill the inbetweens with all kinds of crap and usually get away with it. Look at this example:

Whichever method you use, once your drawings are done, they should have numbers on them. Once you've decided on your layers and numbered your animation, you can make an exposure sheet.

EXPOSURE SHEETS

After that big build up, let me just point out that you *can* get away with not using exposure sheets (or, as cool people in animation say, "x-sheets"; or, as *really* cool people say, "dope sheets"), especially if you build your animation all in Flash.

Below is an example of a *dope* sheet (cuz I'm hella cool), with a simple explanation of how it's used. Essentially, the x-sheet is a way to keep your animation organized—once again, there are times you need order whilst creating chaos.

TITLE:								SCENE #:			PAGE #	
ACTION	DIAL.	9	8	7	6	5	4 ELF	3 SANTA MOUTH	2 SANTA	1 BG	CAMERA INSTR.	FRAME
SANTA GRABS	M											
BLOW TORCH	EH											
AND												
THREATENS												
ELF											START ZOOM IN	
	R											
	EE											
	K											
	R										END ZOOM IN	
	IH											
	SS											
	M											
	SS											

See all those columns? They represent layers of animation. The rows are frames. The column on the far right is *usually* the bottom layer. That's how I work. Some studios put the bottom layer all the way to the left. It doesn't really matter, as long as you're consistent.

Most times, the bottom layer will be your background. The next layers will be your animation. In this instance we have as the next layer our character ("Santa"); above that, his mouth and above that, an elf character.

After your layers is a column for dialogue. Dialogue will be explained in detail later, but for now just know that this column shows the dialogue of your film broken down frame by frame. For example, if you have Santa Claus saying "Merry Christmas," the M might take three frames starting on frame 1, the EH from merry might take another ten frames, etc.

The other spaces on the dope sheet are for camera instructions (such as START ZOOM IN and END ZOOM IN) and descriptions of action (like, "Santa grabs blowtorch and threatens elf").

CHARACTERS

The purpose of this book is not to teach you how to draw or how to create a character. That's your domain—that's where your creativity is in complete control.

But I offer this bit of advice: If you don't want to do lots of work, keep your character very simple. Look at the two drawings below:

The one on the left has pockets, zippers, logos, shoelaces, and all kinds of other crap. The one on the right is much simpler. Why? Because who the hell would want to draw all those zippers and things over and over again every time the character moves? I don't, and you can't make me do it.

ANIMATION LINGO

You've already learned some neat words like "dope sheet" and "inbetween" and "pusillanimous"*; now here are some more words animation pros like to throw around to make outsiders feel insignificant.

ANIMATIC—A filmed storyboard (see below) accompanied by rough dialogue and often sound effects and music. It is used to see if the timing of a film is working. Not essential, but very helpful.

CELS—Thin, transparent sheets of plastic on which animation drawings are traced (or Xeroxed) and painted. Not used much any more, but at one time they were the way almost all 2D animation was made—so much so that 2D is still often called "cel animation."

FIELD—A unit of measurement used in traditional 2D animation. The size of the area on a piece of paper to be filmed is measured in

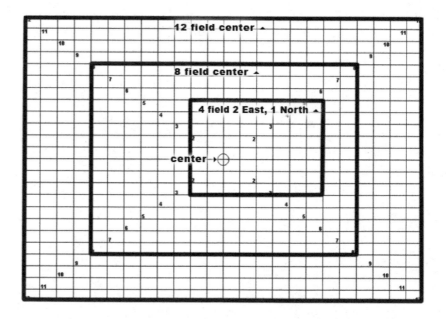

---

*I'm lying. I haven't told you what pusillanimous means and I'm not going to.

fields. Standard animation is done on 12 field paper; if the entire drawing is to be shot, it is said that the shot is "12 field center."

See the illustration on the previous page? The big box is a 12 field center framing. The smaller one is eight field center, and the smallest is four field, two fields east, one field north.

As an independent you don't need to understand this. It is useful when you have someone else shooting your work and you need to put precise camera instructions on your dope (or "x" or "exposure") sheet.

If you don't quite get the concept now, don't worry, it will be discussed more in the layout section.

FIELD GUIDE—A plastic sheet sectioned off in fields so you can plan the framing of your shots.

FOOTAGE—Back before the digital revolution, animation was captured on film. It's not so important to know this anymore, but there are 16 frames in a foot of film, and some animation studios still pay animators by the foot.

INK AND PAINT—In the old days, after drawings were cleaned up, they were traced onto cels in ink and then painted. Today they are scanned into a computer and digitally painted. This process is called DIGITAL INK AND PAINT.

LAYOUT—A drawing of a scene, its background, objects and props, and placement of characters. Animators and background artists both work off the layout.

ONES AND TWOS—If you want your animation to be shot at the rate of one frame per drawing, you are shooting on ONES. If each drawing is exposed for two frames, yes, you guessed it—it's on TWOS. You can also shoot on THREES and FOURS. I've done films where I've shot on NINETY-SIXES.

PAN—Moving the camera across the shot.

PENCIL TEST—Before cleaning up your animation, it's good to film the rough drawings to make sure it's all looking good. This is called a pencil test.

RENDERING—A term from this glorious digital age meaning combining all the elements of your film digitally and outputting them in their final format.

ROTOSCOPING—Tracing live-action footage by hand and using the drawings as animation. This can be done on the computer, and a sophisticated example is the film *Waking Life*.

SCENE—A shot in an animated film. In live-action filmmaking it's called a "shot," but in animation it's a scene. This is only important if you are interacting with animation professionals. Otherwise call it what you want. When I first directed a commercial at a real studio, I was confused by this, since I had learned live-action terminology in which a scene is a collection of shots. Not so in animation.

STORYBOARD—Sort of a comic strip version of your film. Each scene is represented by at least one drawing showing staging and composition.

TRACK READ—After the dialogue for a film is recorded it is analyzed and broken down phonetically, syllable by syllable, frame by frame, on an exposure sheet (as seen earlier this chapter). At a studio, the editor usually does this very tedious job. As a guerrilla animator, most likely you will do it. Be thankful you have access to digital equipment—I used to have to get the sound transferred to film stock and play it through an editing machine. Not fun.

WORKFLOW

You are free to work in whatever order you wish, but this is the sequence of events that usually leads from an idea to a finished film:

1. STORY
2. STORYBOARDS
3. ANIMATIC
4. LAYOUTS/BACKGROUNDS
5. X-SHEETS/ANIMATION
6. PENCIL TESTING
7. SHOOTING (either under a camera or with a scanner)
8. INK AND PAINT
9. RENDERING

HAVE FUN USING THE MEDIUM TO ITS FULLEST

You are working in a very special medium, one where imagination and chaos can reign supreme. So take advantage of it! It's not so easy to do this in live action, is it?

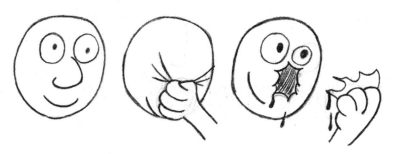

But look, with drawings I did it quite easily. And things can get much worse than that!

Animation Essentials

Most of the concepts in this chapter are missing from much of today's home-grown web animation. By learning the lessons in this chapter, the outsider will be able to bring his or her work to a much more professional level.

ARCS

Most motion in animation—and in real life—follows an arc. Our limbs are on pivots and so travel in arcs:

Gravity and inertia battle each other to make objects traveling through the air follow an arc:

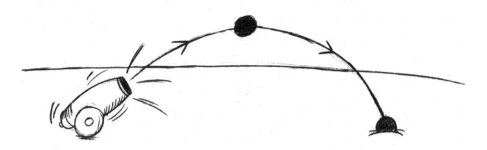

Early in my career I overheard a very well-known and talented animator (who is also a completely self-absorbed jerk) tell a fledgling animator about the importance of arcs. I thought, "This guy's a jerk. What a bastard. He must be wrong. I'll disprove his theory." Well, I couldn't. He was right. Arcs are very important in making motion look nice.

But it turned out to be okay, since it wasn't his theory to begin with—it had been discovered way before his time. And my theory about him being a jerk turned out to be equally valid.

So look at the following illustrations and see how objects and characters move in arcs:

The heel of the foot describes an arc.

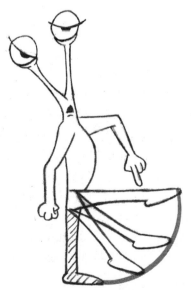

The toe creates an arc.

TIMING

A good sense of timing is what makes a good animator. Twenty-four frames per second is very much a part of timing. Now I will discuss some more refined concepts.

SLOW IN/SLOW OUT

If objects in your animation always move at an even rate, they will tend to look unnatural and uninteresting:

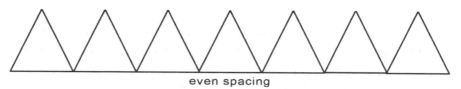

even spacing

Things in real life move at varying speeds, and so should things in your animation.

A simple way to start adding some variance to your timings is to adopt the concepts of "slow in" and "slow out."

"Slow in" means an object moves rapidly as it starts its motion, then slows to a stop. It *slows in* towards its resting place. Here is an example:

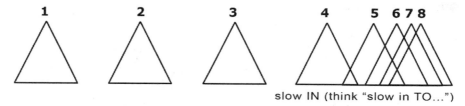

slow IN (think "slow in TO…")

Note how the triangles are spaced: at first they are far apart, then they gradually become denser. Do this as an exercise, either in Flash or on paper. On separate frames draw a triangle, with the spacing I just showed you. Then play it back, with the final triangle held for 24 frames (one second). Note the de-acceleration of the triangle.

Now either draw a new set of triangles with the opposite spacing—that is, densely spaced at first, then further apart—or just shoot your first set of drawings backwards. Again, hold the final triangle for 24 frames. This is called "slow out":

slow OUT (think "slow out FROM…")

See? The triangle moves slowly at first, then rapidly accelerates. It *slowly moves out* of its resting position.

Now look at both sets of animation with each drawing exposed for two frames instead of one. Note the difference in overall timing between ones and twos. As you learn animation, experiment with shooting your drawings on both ones and twos—this will help you get a good feel for timing.

One more exercise. Do an animation that starts slow, speeds up, then ends slow.

slow OUT to slow IN

When you change the spacing of the triangles, here's an easy way to decide how much to change it each time. Look at the slow-in spacing example I gave you. Notice there's a triangle at either side of the frame (triangle 1 and triangle 8). Now notice there's one exactly halfway between the two extremes (triangle 3). And when you're done noticing that, notice there's a triangle halfway between 3 and 8 (triangle 4). And halfway between 4 and 8 you will find triangle 5. 6 is halfway between 5 and 8, and, finally, triangle 7 is halfway between 6 and 8.

Using halfway marks as your spacing guide is a good basic way to plan timing. It will be useful in more advanced animation—NOT ALWAYS, but it's a good starting point.

BOUNCING BALL

What you just learned about slow in and slow out you will now apply to the next exercise, the bouncing ball. Yes, I know, this is all very babyish; why can't you just start making cartoons? Well, you can go ahead, actually. But the knowledge you'll get from these exercises will give your animation more muscle, and perhaps a touch of class.

So, to get to it . . .

Look at the diagram of the bouncing ball:

Notice first the spacing between balls. At the top of the arcs, the spacing is dense. As the ball goes down, the spacing *widens*. When the ball goes back up, the spacing is also wide.

Think about this. Spacing the ball's position like that makes the ball travel at varying speeds—but not randomly so. The ball will gain speed as it falls, quickly accelerate as it goes back up, and lose speed at the top of the arc.

THIS TIMING TECHNIQUE WILL BE APPLICABLE TO MUCH MORE COMPLEX ANIMATION. If you are timing a woman jumping, your animation will conform roughly to this. She will move faster as she descends (the drawings will be spaced farther apart), and as she jumps up she will initially move fast but lose momentum (the drawings will be spaced far apart, then closer). Her movement over the arcs (say she's leaping over a fence) will show deceleration; her spacing in the drawings will be close:

One last thing to note on the spacing. When the ball makes contact, there are two drawings with it touching the ground. (Never mind for the moment that they are shaped differently; we'll get to that in a sec.) The two on the ground give a strong sense that the ball makes contact with the ground. When it takes off in the next drawing, it does not make contact with the ground.

Now, why are the balls all different shapes? This is an exaggeration of natural DISTORTION, which occurs during movement. A real rubber ball won't squash and stretch like this, but it does a little. And by adding it to your drawings, you add life to them. You won't always want to exaggerate this much, but remember the principle. The ball gradually becomes more elongated as it gains speed, gradually less as it loses speed. At the top of the arc it is round. When it strikes the ground it is squashed.

One thing to remember throughout all these deformities is that the ball should retain the *same volume*. That means it should be *very, very loud* all the time.

Actually, I mean "volume" in terms of the space it occupies. So, if you make the ball *longer*, make it *thinner* as well. You don't have to measure it out scientifically, but be conscious of this concept.

By the way, you should also take note of the fact that the second arc is lower and less wide than the first. This is because the ball loses energy as it bounces, so each successive arc will be smaller. That is, if you want to roughly mimic actual physics. Because in a cartoon world, you can do whatever you want. I did a film where one of the characters was a ball and he controlled the height of each of his bounces. You are the Lord God Almighty of your cartoon universe, and as such you create your own laws of physics. Just make sure it looks good or people will hate you.

Now it's time for you to do the exercise. But I won't make you do the simple, boring, baby bouncing ball. You get to do yours with *faces* on it. First, draw a ball following the spacing in the diagram on page 37. Then create a face and set of expressions for the ball.

Be sure to change the expression where it makes sense (such as the point of impact), and don't change expressions a great deal from drawing to drawing.

If you did the first exercise in this book properly (the 24-frames-per-second exercise), you should have an idea of how long something needs to be on screen to make an impression. If the expressions change wildly in every frame, like this:

then no matter how cool each drawing is, the animation will be weak because no single image will register with the viewer.

PENDULUM

If the bouncing ball were Jesus, then the pendulum would be the antichrist, because when it arrives, the world of animation will be annihilated.

Actually, the pendulum is the "anti-bouncing ball" because of the way the drawings are spaced through its arc. Instead of slowing in the arc, the pendulum moves *fastest* through the arc.

By doing this exercise, though it is very basic, you will get used to drawing the arc of your action first and also to timing this kind of action. Think ahead to the animation you *really* want to do. I bet some of you want to have a character punch another character in the face. Well, the punch will follow the basic timing of the pendulum: it will start slow, travel fast in the middle, then slow to a stop at the end.

A punch doesn't have the gracefulness of the pendulum move and is much more extreme in nature, but the timing is similar.

Look at the layout for a pendulum below (note the timing is slow out to slow in):

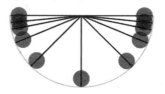

Copy the layout. Note that the timing is spaced in halves like the slow in/slow out timings. If you were animating Tarzan's cousin Louise swinging on a vine, you could use the same basic timing techniques.

Of course, you would want to mess with the timing a bit. Louise might slow out from her first position with more drawings than she uses to slow in at the end. Making the timing uneven this way leads to more natural-looking motion.

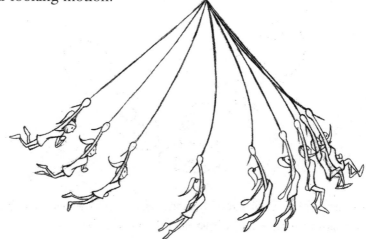

As you get better and more experienced, you will finesse these timings, but these are good defaults to use while you are cranking stuff out.

After copying the layout, do a separate drawing for each position of the layout. Shoot it on ones and twos and compare the results.

WALKING AND RUNNING

Characters walk and run all the time. On the next few pages I will show you basic walk and run cycles that you can copy and adapt to your own characters. For much animation you can use a generic walk or run and get away with it. But if you start doing detailed character animation where the character's walk is meant to help define its personality, you'll be spending a long time getting the walk just right.

However, chances are if you're reading this book, a quick and easy generic walk will suffice, at least for now.

This series of drawings is called a WALK CYCLE. Each drawing will be on a separate sheet of paper. The little line near the feet is for registration; that line goes in the middle of the page. Notice the feet are sometimes in front of it, sometimes behind it, sometimes over it. If you draw the animation like this, your character will look like he's walking in place, which is good for a scene where your character is in front of a moving background:

Notice once a foot strikes the ground it slides backwards in every frame until it lifts, at which point it travels forward in every frame until it strikes again.

The cycle appears in the margins for you to flip and peruse action-wise.

Here is another setup of the same drawings, this time on top of each other. The drawings will be laid out like this if you are doing what is known as a "progressive" animation of the walk. Your character will walk across the screen in this incarnation:

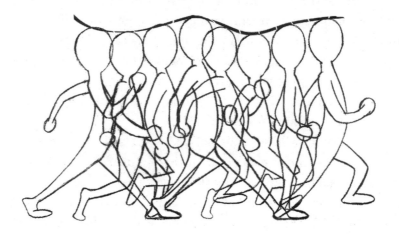

Now, here is a run cycle. In the margin, below the first walk cycle, is a flipbook of the run.

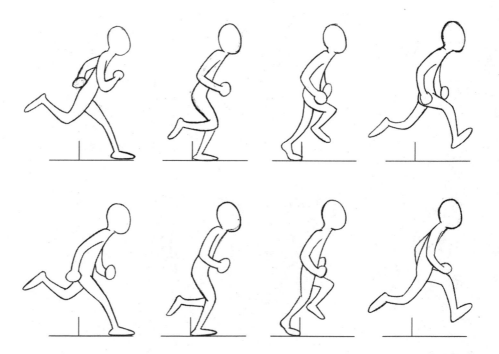

Here's some basic theory on walks and runs:

1. When one foot is forward, the hand on the opposite side of the body is back.

2. Your character's head in a basic walk follows an arcing path, which is indicated in the first illustration on page 42.

3. When someone walks, at least one foot is on the ground at all times.

4. When someone runs, there is a point when neither foot is touching the ground.

5. Walks can be shot on ones or twos with equal success (though the cycles on these pages should be inbetweened if you choose ones).

6. Runs work best on ones.

7. Look at these pictures of my fingers. You can do walk and run cycles with your fingers as models. I find it's a great reference—your fingers work almost exactly like legs.

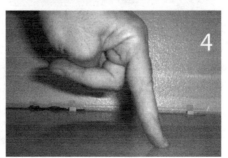

Copy these runs either on paper and shoot them or into Flash and watch them over and over again. Try both the walk and the run on ones and twos. Maybe you like the run on twos; in that case it's perfectly fine for you to shoot it that way—forget what I say if you like it differently.

Very quickly, here's some more advanced info on walks and runs. If you are happy with just copying the drawings I've provided, you can skip this advanced stuff.

Here are selected drawings from the walk cycle, labeled CONTACT 1, DOWN, PASSING, UP, CONTACT 2.

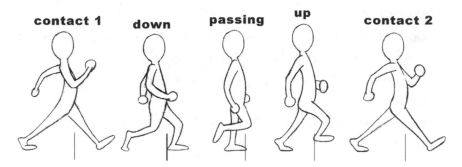

These are the important elements of the walk. Learn these and you can base all sorts of walks on them, depending on what you draw in between them.

You start with two contact poses, making sure that the front foot in one is the back foot in the second. Label the first 1 and the second 5. The contact pose is when the heel of the front foot strikes the ground and the toe of the back foot is all the way back.

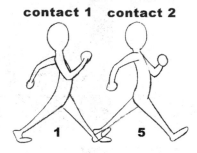

As an inbetween you add the PASSING POSITION drawing. Note that the head is higher than the contact heads. Label this drawing 3. By the way, this is called the "passing position" because it is where the legs pass one another—the one which was in front in CONTACT 1 passes the other leg and becomes the rear leg in the next pose.

Between CONTACT 1 and the PASSING POSE, create a drawing called the DOWN POSITION. The head is lowest in this one. It is drawing number 2.

Between the PASSING POSE and CONTACT 2, you now add the UP POSITION. Here the head is the highest.

You now have five drawings that make up half of your walk. Learn the formula:

1. Start with two opposing CONTACT POSES, drawings 1 and 5.

2. Draw the PASSING POSE between the two contacts (drawing #3).

3. Between CONTACT 1 and the PASSING POSE, draw DOWN POSITION (drawing #2).

4. Between the PASSING POSE and CONTACT 2, draw UP POSITION (drawing #4).

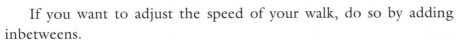

5. Repeat this process, only this time do it using CONTACT 2 as the first drawing and CONTACT 1 as the second. This will give you a complete walk.

If you want to adjust the speed of your walk, do so by adding inbetweens.

To make your walk a cycle, you must make the contact poses in the same spot on your page (see illustration on page 41). Then make the foot that was the front foot in the contact pose *slide backwards* in the passing pose, as the back foot *lifts forward*.

When creating a cycle, between contact poses, the foot that begins at the front *is always sliding back* and the foot that begins at the back *is always moving forward*.

Be careful that you are clear about which leg is the left and which is the right—it's easy to accidentally flip them.

Note the arms in the walk: when the left leg is forward, the left arm is back; when the right leg is forward, the right arm is back. When working fast, you can make the arms reach their extreme position at the same time as the legs. It is simplest to do it like that.

Of course, it's way cooler to have the arms reach their extreme positions on the down pose and the up pose. That way their action is more natural—the arms naturally move looser than the legs and so follow a slightly different timing. This is called OVERLAPPING ACTION, a topic I will discuss very soon.

Here is the walk, with overlapping arm action and inbetweens. It should be shot on ones. Note that the arm motion is much less cartoon-y than it was in the first example.

Chapter 6

DIALOGUE

Below are mouth shapes along with the sounds they represent. You can slap these mouths over any face, in synch with the dialogue, and your character will appear to be speaking.

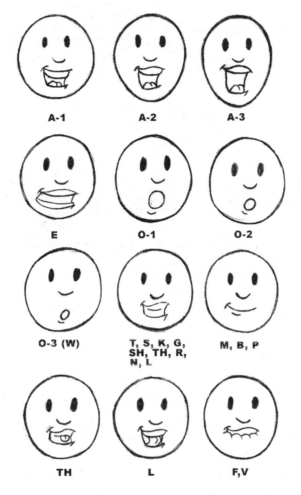

How do you know where to place the mouths? First you have to read the soundtrack. To do this you need a computer program such as Flash or Adobe Premiere that allows you to drag your cursor over the soundtrack, listening to each frame. Some people call this "scrubbing" over the soundtrack.

The next page shows you how to place and read soundtracks in Adobe Flash. If you have another program that allows you to listen to sounds on individual frames (such as Premiere), by all means use it. The benefit of using Flash is that you can add your lip synch animation in the layer above the sound layer and have near-instant gratification.

How to read sound in Flash...

In this example, I will be importing a sound file that is 3 seconds (72 frames) long. So, after opening a new Flash document, I select frame 72 and press F5. This tells Flash my project is 72 frames long.

Next, I go FILE>IMPORT>IMPORT TO LIBRARY:

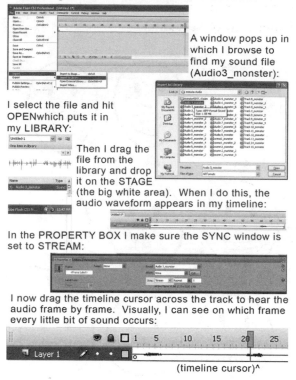

A window pops up in which I browse to find my sound file (Audio3_monster):

I select the file and hit OPENwhich puts it in my LIBRARY:

Then I drag the file from the library and drop it on the STAGE (the big white area). When I do this, the audio waveform appears in my timeline:

In the PROPERTY BOX I make sure the SYNC window is set to STREAM:

I now drag the timeline cursor across the track to hear the audio frame by frame. Visually, I can see on which frame every little bit of sound occurs:

(timeline cursor)^

In the pre-digital era, the dialogue for a film was transferred onto magnetic film stock and was analyzed on a bulky, cumbersome editing setup. Today you can do it on your laptop while riding the bus, if you're that sort of person.

Upon finishing your track read, you will have some very valuable information. You will know on which frame of your film every syllable of dialogue falls. This will allow you to know, for example, that from frames 47 to 53, your character is making an "M" sound and so should have an "M" mouth.

FINESSING DIALOGUE

I know one director who puts all her mouths four to six frames early. She finds it makes the dialogue look more natural. I use a looser method—I usually place consonants, especially Ms and Ps and Bs, two to four frames ahead of the dialogue. I find that when real live people speak they make those mouth shapes before they make the actual sound. But I usually put the vowels right on the money.

Using three O shapes is also useful: the largest one for "Oh" and the smaller two for varying stages of "oo" (refer back to the mouth illustration). I use the Os for Ws as well. And if a character makes the sound

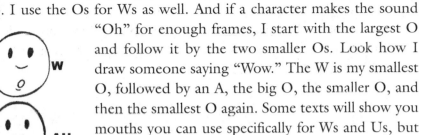

"Oh" for enough frames, I start with the largest O and follow it by the two smaller Os. Look how I draw someone saying "Wow." The W is my smallest O, followed by an A, the big O, the smaller O, and then the smallest O again. Some texts will show you mouths you can use specifically for Ws and Us, but I get by with these Os.

I also find that when swapping mouths over faces, it looks better to keep a mouth on screen for at least two frames. And, especially with fast dialogue, I like to let one mouth shape linger over multiple sounds. For example, if a character says, "Call them!" I might use the K followed by an A followed by an M. Technically, this would spell the word "calm" or "come," BUT when we speak, especially when we speak quickly, we don't really make distinctive individual letter shapes with our mouths.

Dialogue is annoying when you are reading the track, but it becomes fun when you start synching the mouths to dialogue. And if you work in Flash, you can make quick adjustments until you have perfect synch.

SPEED LINES AND SMEAR FRAMES

In order to indicate fast motion, animators often use speed lines and what are known as "smear" frames. See this live-action picture?

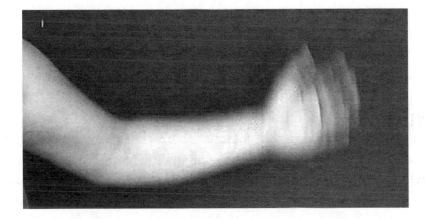

It's blurry because the object was moving while the shutter was open, even though the shutter was only open for an instant.

Because objects sometimes travel faster than a camera can capture them, these blurred frames occur in photographs and in motion pictures. In animation we recreate this effect using what are known as SPEED LINES and SMEAR FRAMES.

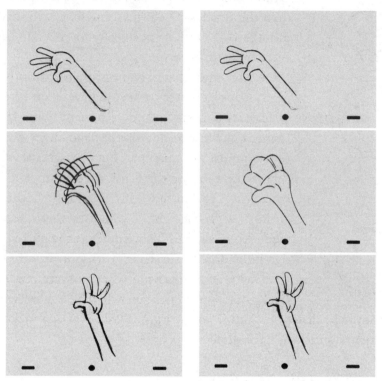

This inbetween uses SPEED LINES.

This inbetween is a SMEAR FRAME.

This isn't done merely because these drawings look cool (though they do); it also helps the eye follow the motion better. The hand in the first drawing of each sequence is quite a distance from the hand in the last drawing; the speed lines and the smear provide a link connecting the two.

Notice both the speed lines and the smear frame follow the arc of the action. In this way they support the flow of the animation.

ANTICIPATION

I know you've been waiting for this section, right? But really, ANTICIPATION is one of the most important concepts in animation. It is lacking in much of the home-grown, underground animation on the web today.

Yet, adding anticipation to your work is easy and absolutely worth your while. The concept is simple: before a character does something, he prepares to do it. He—yes—*anticipates* it. In the illustration in Chapter

One, when the character prepares to kick, that is an anticipation. It can be subtler than that, such as this hand prior to waving.

Before your armed robber reaches into her pocket to pull out her knife, she draws her hand back slightly. An anticipation. Or, as animators

in the know would say, an "antic." (Don't worry—as an outsider you won't have to say things like that.)

On paper, take either an existing character or one of your own and draw it in an anticipation pose and then in a pose of the action. Do several more until you hate me for telling you to do it.

SQUASH AND STRETCH

Like anticipation, SQUASH AND STRETCH is an essential animation concept. You've already used it in your bouncing ball exercise: Your ball stretched as it gained speed and squashed as it struck the ground.

You can use this concept beyond bouncing balls. Look at the man landing and jumping in the following example:

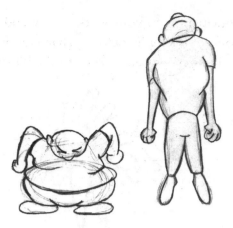

He is squashing and his body contorts. In the next example the character is more realistic and so her body doesn't squash in a rubbery way; instead the squash effect is achieved by her crouching and bending her joints:

When the characters jump in the previous examples, the man stretches in a cartoon-y way, but the realistic woman does so by extending her limbs without any animated exaggeration. Squash and stretch exist in varying degrees of subtlety.

Like you did for anticipation, draw several squash and stretch pictures with a character you like. But don't hate me this time.

SETTLING (OR "CUSHION")

Related to squash and stretch, SETTLING is vital to creating the illusion of motion. Even if done sloppily, adding this will enhance your work.

For example, our character lands and then recoils here. He *settles*. He squashes and stretches as part of it:

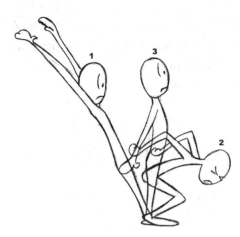

Basically, you want your character to settle after an action such as landing or falling. Here's another wonderful, obstreperous example:

OVERLAPPING ACTION

In good animation, different parts of a character move at different rates. This even happens in bad animation, though the fact that it *does* occur makes said bad animation better than bad animation in which all the parts of a character start and stop at the same time.

That was the best sentence in the book, by the way.

Here's a simple example. Our character on this page is a face. Her name is Helga. In both series of drawings, Helga is surprised by something.

In series A, all her features move at the same rate. In series B, however, first her eyes react while the rest of her face remains unchanged. Then her mouth begins to open. In the last drawings, her eyes have stopped growing but her jaw continues to drop.

Series A   Series B

You could get away with using series A, but series B has more funk, more class, more pizzazz, more nuance. It's a little thing that will help you on your path to excellence.

Here's a second example.

Series A

Series B

Look at Helga's arm. In series A, all three segments (upper arm, lower arm, hand) move at the same rate. That creates very lame, even useless animation. In real motion, the segments of a person's arm move at different rates.

Now note what happens in nice, cooperative, high-achieving series B: The upper arm moves the least, the lower arm moves much more, and the hand moves the most. Check out the starting and ending points of each segment. Notice that the hand is still moving after the other parts have stopped.

Below is another example of where to use overlapping action, and the bottommost flipbook in the margins is a further example.

Hats, hair, and clothes all usually move differently from the rest of the character; they're lighter than the rest of the character and so continue to move and settle after the body has stopped.

From now on, whether you are watching cartoons or real life, make note of overlapping action. Here's one last example, of a girl dancing and turning her head. Notice that the hair keeps moving for many frames after her head has stopped:

The hair also does not repeat the same action forwards and backwards. When something waves or whips, it follows this chart of movement going one way:

and this chart coming back:

This applies to a blade of grass as well as to a ponytail or a tentacle. The object's curve reverses when it comes back.

You *could* repeat the same drawings of the object moving one way when it moves back, but then your animation would be weaker. As a guerrilla animator, that can be acceptable, but with just a little more effort you can raise the level of your animation considerably.

Using this concept will set your work apart from the people who just drag shapes around the screen. Not that there's anything wrong with that—it just sucks.

Promise me you'll at least *think* about it, okay?

DRAWING HANDS

When I was learning to draw, I found drawing hands to be intimidating. I could draw characters pretty well, but the hands would pretty much suck. I would leave them off, avoid them, and otherwise struggle with them.

Then one week I spent an hour every day sketching hands. One day I would do cartoon hands, the next realistic, alternating until I felt comfortable with both. By the end of the week, drawing hands was not only easy for me, it was also *enjoyable*.

One of the great things about drawing realistic hands is that it is an excellent way to do life drawing without having a model. Your own hand is the model and you can pose it in countless ways with easy or difficult perspective.

Below are some guides to constructing cartoon and realistic hands in various positions:

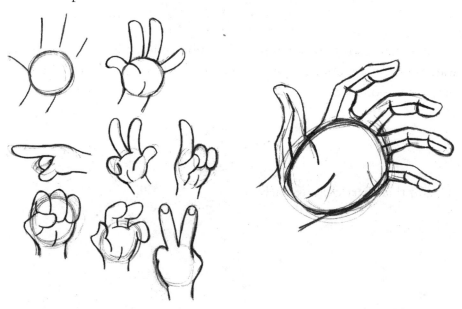

PERSPECTIVE

Like drawing hands, perspective is an aspect of animation that can be intimidating to people who are unfamiliar with it. But, also like drawing hands, the basics are easy to grasp and you can get comfortable with it fairly quickly. Don't fear what you don't know. It's okay to *hate* it, just don't *fear* it.

If you follow your instincts, you will find that you already understand perspective. Things that are far away are small, things that are near are big. I know what you're thinking: "What about ants? Ants are small even when they are near."

But are they? Look at these pictures:

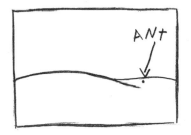 

If you go to art school, in addition to meeting lots of emo kids who smoke, you will learn about VANISHING POINTS, HORIZON LINES, and how to use them to build objects in perspective. "Oh crap," you're thinking, "That sounds BORING!!!" Well, watch me explain it all in *one paragraph*:

Across the middle of your page, draw a horizontal line. That is your HORIZON LINE. Not so hard. Near the left of the page, draw a dot; make another near the right. Voilà! Your VANISHING POINTS. These points are *arbitrary*. Now look how, by using a few more completely arbitrary points, you can construct lines with which you can make 3D shapes:

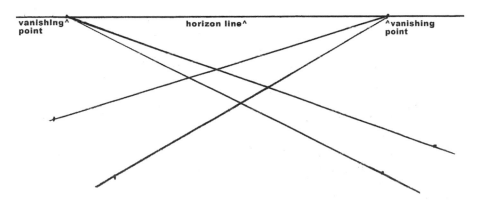

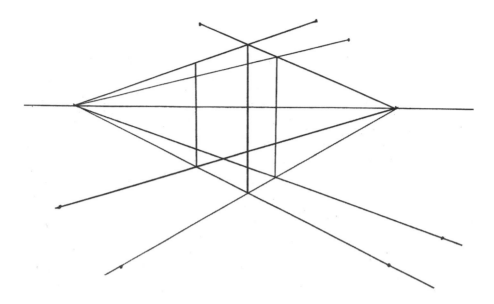

Note how the 3D shapes change in size as they slide up and down the lines. Bigger when nearer, smaller when far away. Just like the ant.

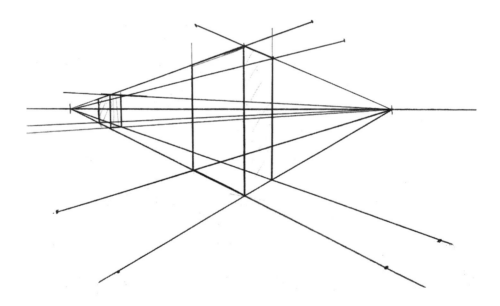

So, one long paragraph and several illustrations later, you now know more about perspective than my Uncle Mike (who doesn't exist).

But what if your characters aren't cubes? How does all this help you? You simply use the cubes as guidelines with which to build your characters. See the next example? The lines and shapes guide you in making your character approach or retreat in perspective:

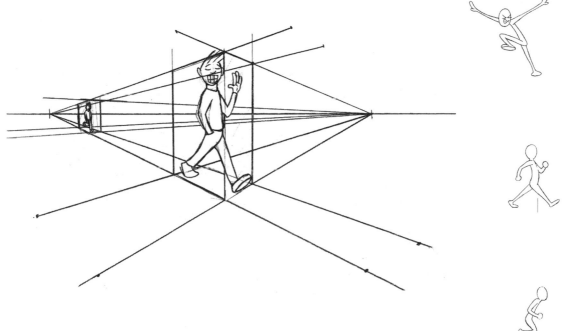

TIMING IN PERSPECTIVE

When a character or object comes towards the camera, not only does he, she, or it become bigger, he, she, or it (h/sh/it) gets closer *faster*. The closer h/sh/it gets to the camera, the faster h/sh/it approaches. So look how I've spaced h/sh/it on h/h/its journey towards or from the camera:

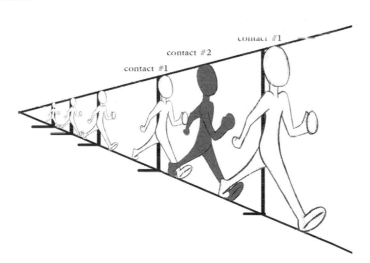

Between each post (where your character is in contact pose 1), h/sh/it will take two steps. Contact 2 occurs between the two contact 1 poses. And of course, between the contact 1 and 2 poses will be passing poses, up and down poses, and inbetweens.

One final bit on perspective: look at this picture and how I have spaced the supports in the highway railing fading into the distance:

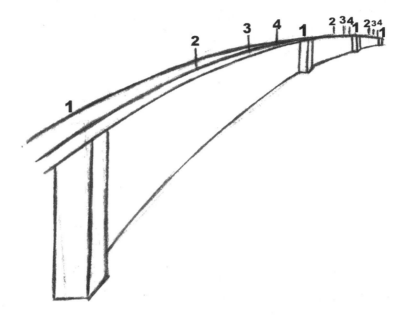

The idea here is that there will be a cycle of four drawings. In drawing one, the posts appear as they do in the illustration. In drawing two, they appear where 2s are indicated, etc.

When drawing rails, fence posts, telephone poles, and other regularly spaced objects going into the distance, use this as your spacing guide every time and you will be okay. To slow the rate of the background movement, add inbetweens.

CHAPTER 7

Animation Cheats

Finally some COOL stuff! Enough of the traditional junk, now let's look at some basic ways to CHEAT!

CYCLES

Since the early days of animation, animators have cheated. CYCLES are one of the oldest methods; they are so old, I already mentioned them in Chapter Five. But allow me to reiterate and expand.

Say you want Helga's brother Sven to wave hello. You draw three pictures of him moving his hand and reshoot them many many times and he will wave for as long as you want him to. In fact, look closely and you will see that Sven's head and body are the same in all three poses. Only his arm moves. In this case, you can cheat further by separating the animation into layers with a non-moving head and body on one level and the moving arms as overlays:

Similarly, this bass-playing monster is a cycle. Three drawings and he grooves forever:

What are some applications for cycles? Besides the aforementioned waving and grooving, you can use them for walking, dancing, writing, stirring a pot—just about anything.

They are also good for background elements such as trees blowing in the breeze, flashing signs, etc.

When planning your animation, always try to think of places you can use cycles (this is advice for guerrilla filmmakers; normal people will want to make lots of beautiful drawings and not use cycles).

REUSABLE EXPLOSION CYCLES

On the pages that follow are drawings of explosion cycles and a smoke cycle. You can use these to end scenes and cover up action. You don't even have to draw them dissipating; in editing you can just fade them out.

Many of the great Warner Bros. cartoons reused explosion and smoke cycles in this way and just faded them out when making the film print, not with drawings.

The drawings from the first explosion cycle can be rearranged at random to create an ever-changing effect.

The second explosion cycle can be used in conjunction with the smoke cycle to make a longer effect where there is a blast followed by smoke, followed by the blast again, etc. To do this, replace the tiny blast in the center of the last explosion drawing with the tiny smoke from the first smoke drawing and let the smoke follow the explosion. When the smoke reaches drawing 8, place the tiny explosion from the second explosion drawing in the center (you can do this by putting

the explosion animation on a layer below the smoke animation) and
let the explosion lead you back to the smoke again:

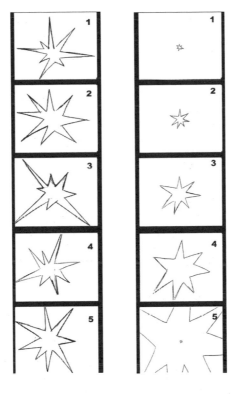

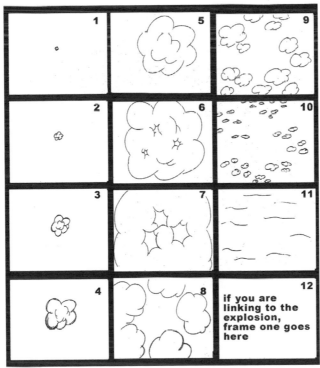

In frame 12: if you are linking to the explosion, frame one goes here

HELD CELS

Of course, if a cycle is too much work, there's always the much simpler HELD CEL. Again, allow me to reiterate and expand. Say your character Miguel is beating up your other character Carmine but, because of a short schedule or tight budget—or even laziness—you don't want to animate the fight. Simply have Miguel start to throw a punch, then cut away to a held cel of Miguel's Uncle Carnaldo cringing in horror. Then the fight can happen off screen while we watch Uncle Carnaldo's one-drawing reaction:

Miguel about to punch Carmine.

Uncle Carnaldo's reaction.

ZIPPING OUT OF THE FRAME

You can make your character exit a frame very simply by ZIPPING OUT. Look at the drawings below.

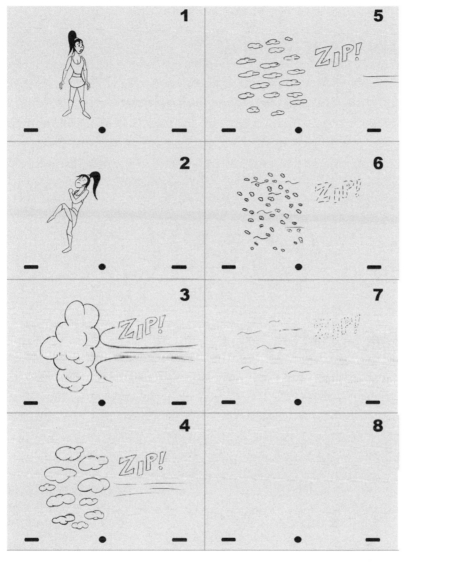

The character is standing in one, in the next she is in an anticipation pose and in the next she is a cloud of smoke with some zippy speed lines. With four more drawings I make the smoke dissipate and home-girl is *gone*.

It's a lot less work than having her walk across the screen, but if you are doing a somber piece about starving children in the third world, this technique will probably seem a bit out of place.

FAKE FIGHTS

If you have characters who are about to fight, you can show them starting to fight, then cut to a series of frames with words like "POW!" and "ZAP!" on them to replace actual animation. This, along with a clever soundtrack, can save you lots of animation time.

CUTAWAYS/REACTION SHOTS

Imagine you have a scene where a character says, "I think I will twist my arm off backwards and beat myself over the head with it, all while riding this unicycle with a trained seal on my back." Instead of animating all that, you could save lots of work and just cut away from the action to a close-up of someone reacting to the described events. Just a few skeptical, disgusted, then finally bored expressions could do the trick.

DIALOGUE CHEATS

As I mentioned in the previous chapter, dialogue can be fun once you have analyzed the track. But it can be very annoying while you are listening to sounds at a frame-by-frame level. So, you can cheat during dialogue. One way is to cut away to another character reacting (as mentioned in the previous paragraph). Here's some other ways:

Any time you use these cheats, you not only don't have to animate dialogue, you also don't have to break down the track first.

LIGHTS OUT

If you can arrange for all the lights to go out in a scene (with the result being that the screen becomes completely black), then you can have all sorts of action take place without animating it, because it's not seen.

Such situations can be extra comical if you use very exaggerated sound effects. A fight after the lights go out, supplemented by bizarre animal noises, screams, and objects breaking, is a sweet little cheat.

OFF-SCREEN ACTION

Closely related to this is off-screen action. Your characters go off-screen, then do something which the audience only hears. Again, incongruous sound effects (or, as the pros say, SFX) help with this.

WALK CHEATS

You *should* get good at walk cycles, but you can avoid them by framing your shots like this, from the waist up:

In Flash and After Effects, you can manipulate one drawing into a walk this way.

Or you could make it so all your characters have wheels instead of feet and create a show called *The Wheelers*.

HI, I'M TIMMY WHEELER!

But you might want your work to be successful, in which case don't do that.

Animation Cheats

Here is a scene starring a character of mine named Kellogg the Invisible Duck. Note how simple he is to animate since he's invisible:

CAMERA MOVES

If your camera is very active, it can make up for a lack of animation. Just panning over a background will add life to what is otherwise a still frame.

Keeping the camera roaming around and slightly restless gives your work a constant sense of motion. In live-action the camera is rarely still, even if it appears to be.

Back in the pre-digital age, moving the camera a lot was difficult and slowed shooting down (making it more expensive). Now, with programs such as After Effects, it's easy and inexpensive to let your camera roam around a shot.

RE-PEGGING

This is not really cheating, but it is very useful, though perhaps not so obvious.

Say you animated the following two drawings:

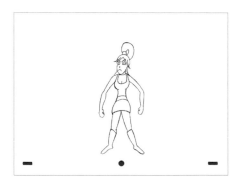 

Now, what if you decided the last drawing should be further to the left than you drew it? Should you cry? Should you draw it again? Or should you merely RE-PEG it?

If you choose to re-peg it, simply cut your animation paper, separating the top from the peg holes, like so:

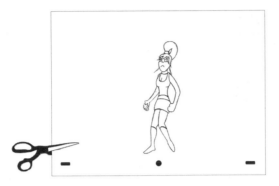

Then, placing the strip with the peg holes back on the peg bar, move the severed portion of the art to the left where you want it, then tape it back to the strip with the peg holes:

There will be times when you will want to do this to multiple drawings; doing so will save you from redrawing everything.

ART CHEATS

Much of the art that critics and historians call the greatest of all time is very old. Which, to the independent animator, should mean one thing—you can use it for free! Using bits of these paintings by Manet, Pissarro, and del Verrocchio:

I took the highlighted tree from this Bow Wow Wow cover painted by Manet . . .

Pissarro provided the road and buildings . . .

The sky came from another Manet painting . . .

And del Verrocchio chipped in with this tree.

I made this entirely new background:

And note how I made no jokes about the name Pissarro.

PHOTOGRAPHIC CHEATS

Look at this photograph and compare it to the three versions of it that follow:

Cut-out filter

Paint daub filter

Palette knife filter

All I did was apply Adobe Photoshop filters to the original in order to give them an artistic overtone.

Using Photoshop filters straight up, however, can become monotonous. But by combing filters and effects, you can create a new style and look. This background here is made of elements I took from several photos, doctored in Photoshop, then assembled as a new piece of art for use as a background:

TURNING CHARACTERS AND THINGS AROUND

Look at this character named Esmerelda. In the first set of drawings, she is turning her head by way of several drawings:

Lots of work, yes? Well, not so much, but perhaps more than you want to do.

Esmerelda could also turn her head like this:

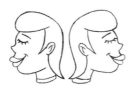

This method uses the same drawing, reversed in the computer. On screen it will be an extremely cartoon-y flip from one position to another, but it will work. And if you want to funk it up a little bit more, add a frame like this:

This frame acts as a quick link between the flipped drawings and gives your animation a bit of an edge over animation done with just a simple reversal of drawings.

Notice that in the transitional frame, Esmerelda's line of action follows a slight arc; Esmerelda's face does not merely move side to side. Arcs make animation better.

By the way, do you recognize the method used in this transitional frame? It was discussed in Chapter Six under "smear frames."

COPYING FROM THE MASTERS

One of the many privileges of living in the digital age is that you can steal so many things. If you have a scene of classic animation you want to copy (or just study in depth), digitize it from DVD, make it into a file After Effects can read (Quicktimes and AVIs are good), bring it into After Effects, export each frame as a jpeg sequence, print them out, and you will be able to trace the action over onto blank paper, using your own characters.

Usually this method is best just as reference, but sometimes you might want to completely steal something outright.

In the chapters on After Effects and Flash I will show you more cheats, such as how to add squash and stretch to drawings, how to quickly add tones and highlights to your characters, and a bunch of other ways to make very few drawings do the work of many.

KEEP A REUSABLE LIBRARY

Keep a library of finished animation-leg cycles, eye blinks, trees, birds flying-things you can reuse in the future. You might create a scene one day that needs an added element and, if you have a well stocked library, you could, for example, pull out a walk cycle of a cat, pop it into the background, and give your scene an extra bit of quality.

CHAPTER 8

Storyboards, Layouts, Backgrounds, Animatics

Once you, the animator, have learned to make things move well, you must then figure out how to visualize a story as well as design and execute the world in which your story takes place. That is what storyboards, layouts, backgrounds, and animatics involve.

STORYBOARDS: AN OVERVIEW

The simplest explanation of a storyboard is that it's like a comic strip version of your film. You take your idea and sketch little pictures of each important thing that will appear in the final movie.

For example, here's my story: a monster finds a box on the sidewalk of a deserted street. He picks up the box, looks at it, and then it suddenly explodes in his face. As he stands covered in soot, another monster peeks out from behind a trash can, laughing. When the first monster sees her, he says, with quiet anger, "Very funny, Mom."

Now, here's my storyboard (or simply "board," as the hip industry people whom we hate would say) for the script:

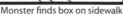
Monster finds box on sidewalk   He lifts box

He reacts happily

SFX: BOOM!!

Laughter from off screen

Mom Monster is laughing

Monster: "Very funny Mom!"

Notice I've mixed close-ups with wide shots and used slightly skewed camera angles. That's all my choice. There are many ways I *could* have staged the story, but this is what I decided to do. The point is, I figured out my camera angles and the staging of my characters, and now the storyboard will serve as a blueprint for my animation.

Storyboard Composition

Imaginative composition makes the difference between an inspired board and an average one. Here's a rather dull way I could have told the same story:

Monster finds box on sidewalk

He lifts box

SFX: BOOM!!

Laughter from off screen

Monster: "Very funny Mom!"

THUMBNAILS

Thumbnails are quick, tiny sketches which are often created prior to the actual storyboard. I prefer doing thumbnails first because I can work fast and sloppy to get my ideas down on paper. Here is a thumbnail version of the above story:

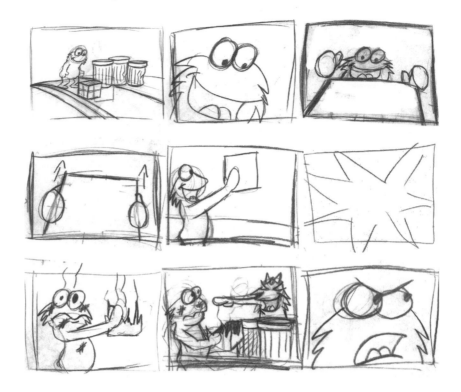

Sometimes all you need is your thumbnails. If you are working by yourself and the thumbnails are sufficient for you to know how to proceed, then there's no need for you to make a more formal storyboard.

INSPIRATIONAL SKETCHES

Prior to creating layouts and backgrounds, artists make inspirational sketches as they feel their way towards a final look. This is a time to have fun, especially if you don't have a deadline. Go crazy designing your movie to be everything you've always wanted to make. Then sit down with all your sketches later and figure out whether you can actually *do* it, or, more importantly, if you *want* to do it.

BACKGROUNDS: CHOOSING A STYLE

There are many factors involved in choosing a background style: budget, deadline, type of story, style of animation, and your artistic fortes are the most important.

If you have lots of time and are a brilliant watercolor painter, then perhaps you'll do all original watercolors.

If you are in a hurry or not good at painting, perhaps you'll use photographs which you manipulate in Photoshop to look like original art (as discussed in Chapter Seven).

MOVING BACKGROUNDS

The simplest type of moving background is one I'm sure you have already figured out how to make. It's the kind you see in *Scooby Doo* and *The Flintstones*: the long background that moves left to right or right to left, usually repeating itself many times.

But in case you haven't figured it out, here's how it's done: You make a background that is longer than your screen size and then make the last part of it exactly the same as the first. (It's easiest if the first and last parts are as wide as your screen.) Here's an example:

LAYOUTS

If you are directing something and handing scenes off to other animators, you should make layouts so the animators know what to do. But if you are working on your own, only do a layout when you need to.

Referring back to the storyboard above, consider the scene where the monster looks at the box in his hands. I might just go right ahead and draw that scene without bothering with a layout. It would most likely be a HELD FRAME (that is, with no movement going on in the shot), so drawing a layout and then making an animation drawing would be redundant.

Now look at the panel where the mom pops out laughing. For that shot, I *would* make a layout because I need to plan where the trash cans from whence she emerges will be. If I base my background and my animation off of the layout, then I will be sure that my characters match up with background elements.

Only, the trash cans might not be part of the background. Most likely I would make them an OVERLAY so that I could put the mom animation *over* the background but *under* the cans, over all of which would go the original monster character. Note the illustrations:

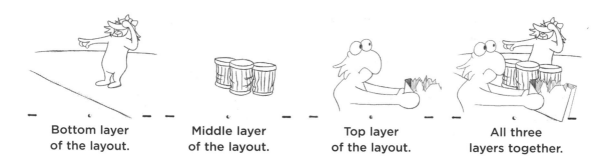

| Bottom layer of the layout. | Middle layer of the layout. | Top layer of the layout. | All three layers together. |

Seem confusing? This is where x-sheets are useful—to keep track of what goes on what layer. Here is an x-sheet notating this scene:

ACTION	10	9	8	7	6	5	MONSTER 4	CANS 3	MOM 2	BG 1	CAMERA INSTR.	FRAME
							1		1	1	4f, 3 fe/2fn	1
												2
									2			3
												4
									3			5
												6
									4			7
												8
									5			9
												10
									4		START CAMERA MOVE	11
											FROM 4 f, 3fe/2 fn	12
									3		to 10 f/c	13
												14
									2			15
												16
									1			17
												18
									2			19
												20
									3			21
												22
									4			23
												24
									5		END CAMERA MOVE	25
												26
									4			27
												28
									3			29
												30
									2			31
												32
									1			33
												34
									2			35
												36
									3			37
												38
									4			39
												40
									5			41
												42
									4			43
												44
									3			45
												46
									2			47
												48

Whether the cans are part of the background or an overlay, I know where to put them because of the layout.

PLOTTING A CAMERA MOVE IN YOUR LAYOUTS

Wow, now this is advanced stuff! This is for when you're so successful with your own films that somebody hires you to do a big project with a budget and you have to make layouts for other artists to work from. If you are in a hurry to make a movie, skip this bit for now and read it when you have people working for you.

Still here? Okay, look at this slightly altered version of the layout:

I'm sure you noticed the box around the monster's head from which four arrows extend. This indicates that the scene will start out with a close-up of the monster (the area encompassed by the box), then the camera will pull out to show the full frame.

But what, you might ask, are the cryptic notations on the layout? What is this "4f, 3 fe/2 fn" with a plus sign beside it in the middle of the small framing and this "10 f/c" next to a plus sign in the center of the page?

Those, dear reader, are CAMERA INSTRUCTIONS. They are written in a notation first introduced in Chapter Five of this very book. The first bit means "four field, three fields east, and two fields north." The second bit means "ten field center."

A FIELD is a unit of measurement in animation. These instructions on the layout are saying that the shot starts out at a size called "four field" and is centered on a spot that is three fields to the east (or right) of the center of the page, and two fields north (or above) the center of the page. By the end of the shot, the shot will be at a size called "ten field," with the center of the shot being the center of the page.

To make this even clearer, here is the layout with a FIELD GUIDE superimposed over it—from this you can do the math and see that I'm not lying:

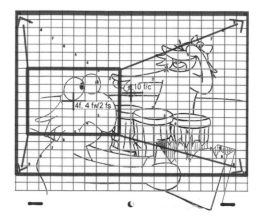

Note that the four field box is eight units wide and eight units tall, and that the ten field box is 20 units wide and 20 units tall. If a shot is "4 field" that means there are four fields to the north, south, east, and west of the center; hence it is eight fields wide but called 4 field.

On your x-sheet, in the column called "camera instructions" you put down the information about field sizes. In our example, the shot starts out at 4 field, 4 fields west, 2 fields south of center, for ten frames. At frame 11 a very fast camera move begins (15 frames long, just over half a second) bringing the camera to a "10 field center" position for the rest of the scene.

Between the x-sheet and the layout, you will know how to animate and shoot the scene; you will know that until the zoom-out occurs, nothing outside of the four-field area will be visible and so will not have to be animated.

LAYERED LAYOUTS

The layout in the previous example is broken into separate layers. But I could have done it all on one layer. More layers sometimes make it easier to understand the scene, but they are not always necessary.

DANGER!

When making layouts, please remember one more thing: *stuff at the edges gets cut off!!!* If you work with a field guide, look at where the action-safe lines are and work within these. Otherwise, give yourself a one-inch margin all the way around your paper and make sure anything important is inside the margins.

Why? Because when your work goes to film or TV or DVD, inevitably the edges get cropped. Programs like After Effects have field guides so you can check yourself before you wreck yourself. Remember, if you forget this and draw out to the edges of your paper, you will lose stuff!!!

A well-planned scene that didn't get cropped.

A poorly planned scene that suffered the consequences.

ANIMATICS

An animatic is a filmed version of your storyboard. When creating it, you must decide how long to leave each scene on screen. You can decide this by guessing, using a watch or stopwatch and timing each scene as it plays in your imagination, or by preparing the soundtrack ahead of time and matching the storyboard to that.

Usually I have at least a rough soundtrack to go with the animatic, composed of a dialogue track, some rough sound effects, and sometimes even a temporary music track.

The purpose of the animatic is to give you a sense of how your film is going to look before you spend time doing all the animation. Animatics often reveal timing changes you might need or whether or not shots flow properly into one another, and they let you get an overall feel of how the final version will play.

You can make your animatic with Adobe Premiere, Final Cut Pro, FlipBook, Adobe After Effects, or any video editing software you like. If you don't know how to edit, it's easy to learn.

CHAPTER 9

Cheating with Storyboards, Layouts, Backgrounds, and Animatics

There's not too much cheating to be done on storyboards other than drawing very sketchily and copying and pasting panels that will be reused.

However, you can cheat by parlaying your storyboard into layouts. If planned properly, the same drawing can be used for a storyboard panel, a layout, and even a background. In 1940, while on a tight budget and deadline for their film *Dumbo*, the great and powerful Walt Disney Company used this very cheat, though not all the time, nor to the extent that it can be utilized. And they only used storyboards for layouts; they didn't take things so far as to turn them into backgrounds.

Even if your storyboard frame is very small, if it's drawn well you can blow it up to layout size and use it.

And if you make your layouts with several layers, as discussed in the previous chapter (i.e, the background is separate from the characters, etc.), then the background level can be scanned and painted and used as a background, and the character levels can even serve as key drawings for your animation.

Also, as discussed in Chapter Seven, by using Photoshop filters you can turn photographs into watercolor paintings or even cartoon-y backgrounds.

Character and Story Cheats

If you believe your story is good, then it *is* good. If your characters are alive in your head, then they are real. You know a character is "alive" when you can think of any situation and immediately know what your character would do in it.

There are many books on screenwriting that list rules and regulations regarding how to structure your screenplay, but these books are to art what the SATs are to knowledge. They are useful if what you want to do is play within the system.

Executives within said system most often approach stories with a patriotic allegiance to these rules. They will read a script then say things like, "What has your character learned by the end of the story?" and "You need to endear your character to the audience." But what's wrong with a story about an un-endearing total bastard who learns absolutely nothing? Why, he could be the head of a major motion picture studio!

Because you are reading this particular book, I assume you are not of that mind-set. So what I have to say about story and characters will be brief.

You should be making a film because you want to say something or because you want to make some noise or because you want to offer an alternative to the mainstream. Therefore you most likely know what you want to say already.

Here are some mottos to consider:

- If you please yourself with your film then at least one person will think it's great.

- Never be boring.

- Never censor yourself. Well, maybe if—no, no, never.

- Don't be afraid to be slow or subtle or intelligent—these terms are not synonymous with boring.

Carry some sort of notebook with you at all times, along with a pen or pencil. Inspiration will strike you in the strangest of places, and if you don't get it on paper, you may lose it forever. This is true at all times but especially true when you are in the middle of creating a project.

Keep this notebook and pencil by your bed so you can write down dreams as well. Some of the best ideas come from dreams, but if you don't write a dream down immediately, you almost always forget it very quickly.

As you get deeper into shaping your film, ideas will come to you at a greater rate and volume. You must keep pace with them and get them down on paper somewhere. You can text message yourself or leave yourself voicemails, but as an animator, often your ideas will require sketches. So always be ready.

At some point, all these notes will reach a critical mass and be ready to be transformed into a cohesive story. When you feel you have reached this point, start to organize the notes and don't be afraid to leave something out, *even if it's a great idea*. Sometimes an idea will be fantastic but detract from the overall story. It's painful, I know, but learn to cut such scenes. And don't despair: they usually become useful in a future project.

Also, if something seems like a great idea when you first conceive it but later when you tell people about it they go, "Um, yeah, whatever," don't give up on it. You may have presented it badly, they might be jealous of the idea, or—most likely—they just can't visualize it.

So many times people have given me lukewarm responses to ideas but have loved the final film. Why? Because the finished film filled in all the blanks for them. When I told them the idea, they couldn't see all the things I saw in my head. But when the film came out, they got it, because I showed them what I meant.

Excuse the shocking image, but oftentimes telling people about an idea before you've completed it is like ripping a fetus out of the womb and waving it around and saying, "Isn't this going to be a beautiful baby?!" People need to see the *actual* baby. Believe in your fetus, but maybe don't show it to everybody.

Sometimes too you will get sick of an idea and think it's terrible. However, this might be a case of you having worked too closely with it.

If so, you may just need a break. Don't be afraid to step away from a project for a couple of weeks if it gets stagnant. When you return, chances are you will remember why it excited you to begin with.

WHERE THE CHEATS ARE

If you are an independent animator, a rebel, a GUERRILLA, chances are you have plenty of story ideas and this book is useful to you only as a way of making said ideas happen.

But if you feel the need to cheat when coming up with a story, you'll find you've got some very famous company.

William Shakespeare and Walt Disney both took all their plot ideas from preexisting sources. And so can you! In fact, you can make the same exact stories they did, because nobody owns those stories. Snow White. Romeo and Juliet. Pinocchio. Lennon and McCartney. All these legendary tales are in the public domain, which means that YOU can use them for FREE. Except maybe for Lennon and McCartney. As a matter of fact, you'd probably get sued rather completely if you used them. In fact, if I'm not careful . . .

Anyway . . . you could, if you so desired, animate the complete works of Shakespeare, word for word, and not get sued. And it could be funny, too, especially if you did it like this:

The lovely cast of King Lear.

And think of all the famous characters you can use! Santa, Satan, Jesus, God, Abraham Lincoln, Uncle Sam, Auntie American, the aforementioned Snow White, the immediately-about-to-be-mentioned Cinderella, Peter Pan. You get the idea, right? You can even make a film about how Abraham Lincoln and Cinderella challenge Peter Pan to a miniature golf contest—though really, why would you?

However, you *do* need to be careful when using these properties. For example, if you make a Pinocchio movie, make sure you base it on the original book, not the Disney film. Disney's Jiminy Cricket does not exist in the book—and they could sue you for that. Likewise, if you use the seven dwarves, remember that their names in the Disney film were given to them by Disney writers. If you do Peter Pan, make sure Tinker Bell is a point of light, not a tiny woman in a skimpy dress—once again, the latter version was created by Disney.

CHAPTER 11

Effects

In the 1930s, animators at Walt Disney Studios began to specialize. One of the specialties was EFFECTS, things like fire, lightning, rain, snow, wind, water, and vomit. Who can forget that scene in *Snow White* where Grumpy vomits in the soup but doesn't tell anyone and they all eat it? Coool!

The quickest and easiest way to put effects in a film is if you have After Effects. After Effects has filters for lightning, lens flares, glows, etc., and you can buy plug-ins for snow and rain.

There is another piece of software called Particle Illusion, which allows you to quickly and easily generate many effects such as rain, lightning, shadows, smoke, kaleidoscopes, and more, which you can then import into your After Effects projects.

Particle Illusion is very easy to figure out and is relatively inexpensive.

DRAWING EFFECTS

But if you don't have the above-mentioned programs or just prefer the look of hand-drawn effects, below are examples of snow, rain, and simple waves.

Explosions and smoke explosions, as you may remember, appeared earlier in the book.

SNOW

Snow looks best when it doesn't fall straight down. It should follow a graceful path. The best way to create a snow cycle is to plan out paths for several flakes to follow, then make a chart indicating how far the flakes progress between each drawing. Here is such a chart:

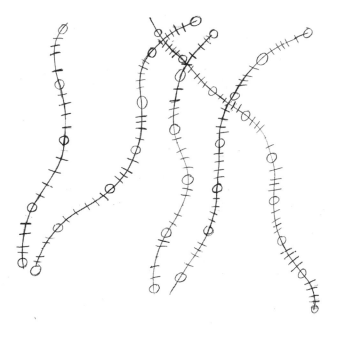

Each circle represents the first flake in the cycle. The lines show that four more drawings follow before the cycle returns to the beginning.

Here are five snow cycle drawings based on the chart:

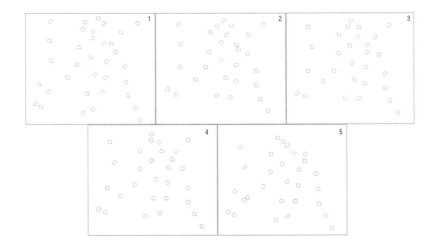

RAIN

Here is a basic four-drawing rain cycle:

LIGHTNING

A lightning effect can be achieved many ways. Just having the screen go completely white for a few frames (with an accompanying thunder sound effect) will work. Or you can do something like this:

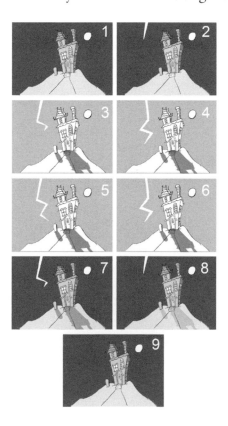

You might have noticed that when the bolt strikes, the sky and the house get lighter and a shadow falls across the lawn. That helps the effect.

Also, in this case the bolt grows quickly and then inverts its shape a couple of times. This is a very simple, cartoon-y way to do it. You can, if you wish, make the bolt grow and fork more elaborately.

When adding the thunder sound effect, add it simultaneously with the picture (or just three or four frames later). While in real life, unless you are actually getting struck by lightning, there is a delay between the flash and the rumble, in most cases your effect will be more vibrant and believable if the sound and picture coincide.

WAVES

This cycle is a nice quick way to add wave motion to a body of water. Place a few copies of it, in various sizes, at different spots in your water:

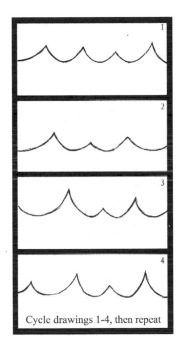

Cycle drawings 1-4, then repeat

CHAPTER 12

Sound

Music, dialogue, and sound effects are hugely important in animated filmmaking, *especially* when cheating. A great music track, funny dialogue, and clever use of sound effects can compensate for very limited animation.

CLEVER WAYS TO USE SOUND

How you decide to use sound will determine how it adds or detracts from your picture. In addition to being an animator, I happen to also be a musician. As a result, sound and picture have always been of equal importance to me. Over the years my thoughts on the subject have grown from vague theories to specific techniques, which I will now share with you.

A STEADY, INFECTIOUS BEAT

If there is a nice beat on your soundtrack, perhaps with a bass line, one that makes people's heads bob, it will drive your film's story and allow you to skimp on the animation, especially if you make your edits to the beat.

Sometimes a rhythm that's just on the borderline between catchy and annoying actually works best. But a catchy song is even nicer. If the music engages the audience, they won't notice deficiencies in your animation. Not that I'm saying you will have deficiencies in your animation. But you will.

HOME STUDIOS VS. PROFESSIONAL STUDIOS

I do most of my sound recording at home. The software I use is called Cubase, but there are many you can use that are very similar, such as Pro Tools, Reason, Cakewalk, etc. And if you don't plan to create your own music, simpler software will suffice.

Since I do create music, though, I use a top-notch program.

However, the fact remains that I record in my own home and what I create is of good enough quality to be broadcast on major networks and played in major theaters in major cities of major nations.

There's no point in going to a studio and paying by the hour if you have decent home-recording software. When I prepare something for broadcast or theatrical release, however, I do take my final mix to a studio to be mastered.

MASTERING is the process by which the frequencies in your mix are tweaked subtly to brighten the brights and punch up the lows. The overall volume is usually made to be fairly uniform, and everything is brought up to broadcast standards.

I do not do this at home for two reasons. One, I do not have expensive studio speakers on which to listen, and two, I prefer to pay someone who masters for a living to get the sounds right. For a short project (30 seconds to five minutes), a professional engineer can usually have everything sounding nice and sweet in less than an hour.

BUY A GOOD MICROPHONE

Unless you don't mind the crappy quality of cheap computer mics (or headset or camcorder mics), you should spend a little bit of money on a decent microphone for voices. A Shure SM58 or a Sennheiser E98 will suffice and, if you go to a discount music house or online store, you can get one for a little over $100.

Like I said, if you don't mind the crappy sound, don't bother. But I personally like my work to stand apart from the pack, and clean audio helps.

VOICE-OVER (CHOOSING AND DIRECTING TALENT)

Ah, yes, recording voices. If you have good actors, your film will shine. But if you use your stupid, untalented friends who do really bad "announcer" voices, your film will sound like you made it with your stupid, untalented friends.

So start hanging out with smart, talented people. Failing that, consider hiring people to do the voices (again, avoiding stupid, untalented ones).

When directing your actors, make sure you know what you want so you'll know it when you hear *them* do it. Be able to do any line for your talent in order to demonstrate the delivery you want. AND, make sure you get the performance you want—don't settle for "almost." If you let "almost" good things into your films, your work becomes mediocre. And once you let one "almost" good thing in, you start letting in more and more. I know. I've done it before. I've wanted to get things done so I've "lived with" sub-par performances and regretted it later.

Sometimes an actor will have a way of delivering a line that differs from your vision but is still good. Record that version as well—later you might find that it's actually better than your idea. But make sure you also get what you want. Then, as you edit, you can decide what you like best.

If you think your actor has nailed the line on his or her first try, then MOVE ON. Many producers insist on "getting a safety," which means they make the actor do the line again "just in case." "Getting a safety" is just filmspeak for "I have no spine and don't trust my own judgment so I'm going to annoy the talent by wasting their time." If you let your actors know that you trust their talent by doing only one take when they nail it, it increases their confidence.

Also, if you spend all day getting safeties, you will bore and tire your actors. You're boring me already, just making me think about it . . .

HOW TO GET A GOOD RECORDING

In this wonderful digital age, we have so many advantages over the old fashioned, primitive analog world of yesterday. But in sound recording, digital is much less forgiving than analog when it comes to tracks being ruined by distortion.

To put it simply, if you record something too loud with digital technology, the take will be ruined. So, rule number one for getting a good recording is WATCH YOUR LEVELS.

The flipside of this is to make sure your levels are loud enough. If what you record is barely louder that the ambient noise in the room, then as you increase the overall volume, the ambient noise will be very noticeable.

Make sure your recording space is adequately soundproofed or that you record at a time when you won't get lots of neighborhood noise on your takes.

In addition to the above technical points, there are many artistic things you can do to get a good recording.

1. Make sure your actors are comfortable performing. If an actor is cramped at the microphone, or the mic is at the wrong height, it will affect the performance.

2. Always encourage your talent. If you don't like a take, don't be negative; just keep going after one you like. And when the take is perfect, be effusive in your praise.

3. If the actor is having trouble with a particular line, it is sometimes wise to leave it and move on. You can always come back to it later.

4. Also, if the actor is struggling with a line, sometimes it helps to just keep recording one long take instead of stopping and starting again and again. Let him or her try it fifty times in a row, uninterrupted.

SCORING AND RECORDING MUSIC

If you use music written and performed by someone other than your-self, you will need to get permission from the copyright holder (which will most likely cost money) before you can sell your work. If you are only going to show your cartoon to your friends, you don't need to get permission.

However, if you have grand plans for global distribution, you might want to use original music. This can be either composed and performed by you yourself (if you have such skills), by a friend (if she has such skills), or, if you are in college, by a music major in your school. You will find many budding composers in colleges who need to hone their skills, and practicing on other students' films is a perfect way for them to do this.

PUBLIC DOMAIN MUSIC

There is music you can use in your film for free: classical music or old music for which there is no copyright. This music is considered to be in the public domain, which means that anyone—even you—can use it.

However, while the *music* is available, a specific *recording* of it won't be. So you will have to play it yourself or find someone to play it for you.

EDITING MUSIC

Now I will tell you an amazing secret to putting music to film: Drop any song behind any picture and all sorts of things are going to synch up as if you meant for them to happen. Perhaps you've heard the rumor that Pink

Floyd wrote *Dark Side of the Moon* as a score to the *Wizard of Oz?* The reason it seems true is because of what I just said. Try it sometime. Just randomly play music with various bits of film. Cool things will happen.

So, when editing music, you *could* do a painstaking cutting job, but you might want to see what chance provides you first.

CREATING SOUND EFFECTS

There are many CDs with sound effects available for purchase, and these make a very nice starting point for adding effects to your films. In the business, these are generally referred to as "library effects," though they sound nothing like a library at all.

However, creating your own effects can be fun and rewarding, and also allows you to have sounds on your film that no one else has.

Sometimes you will have to create an effect because you can't find what you want on CD. Once I made a film where a Mafia reindeer broke the antler off another reindeer's head. It may surprise you, but I had nothing like this in my sound effects library, so I spent about ten minutes snapping plastic CD cases in half in front of a microphone until I had a collection of crisp snapping sounds. I layered a couple together and got the nice, sickening *crack* I wanted.

ALTERING AND AUGMENTING SOUND EFFECTS

Once you've gathered all your effects, IMPROVE THEM. It's what *real* sound people do, so why not at least try it? For example, say you have a character shoot a gun. Instead of just putting a library effect of a gun on the soundtrack, try putting three or four at the same time. It makes a bigger, heavier sound.

And if you're doing a funny film, put incongruous sounds in as well. Along with the three gunshots, add a pig squealing. Or Richard Nixon muttering. (Richard Nixon makes everything funnier.)

If someone gets punched, add a bowling strike to the punch effect.

Making crashes obnoxiously over the top in terms of volume and intensity makes them funnier. I like to use shattering glass even when there is no glass involved. Breaking glass is just funny. Next time you're in a restaurant or a department store, start smashing glasses and see if I'm not right.

CHAPTER 13

Flash

Adobe Flash is a big, bad, often confusing program that nevertheless is widely used in animation today. This chapter, along with the subsequent After Effects chapter, is filled with detailed exercises to help you and these programs get along.

If you wish to read the rest of the book first and then come back to these two chapters, that's okay. It will be better if you don't rush through this part but instead pay attention and absorb all the tools and techniques offered by the software.

Instead of lots of exposition and explanation, I'm going to give a series of tutorials that will get you to the point where you can use Flash for production animation.

But first, some basics.

1. MAKE SURE YOUR FLASH DOCUMENT IS SET AT 24 fps. You do this in a little box at the bottom of the timeline which opens a bigger box for you. Also in this box, set the dimensions of your project. Unless you have a reason not to, make it 720 pixels wide, and 480 high (standard television size).

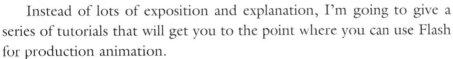

double click this to change frame rate

2. Make sure you remember where and what the TIMELINE is! (It's the window at the top of your Flash page with the numbers indicating frames and layers on the left.)

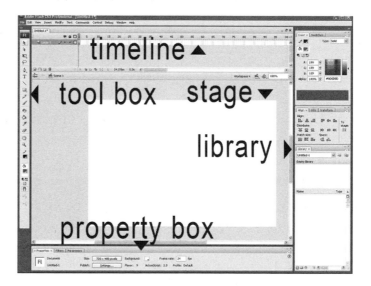

3. STAGE: the big white area in the middle of the page. This is where you create your animation. Whatever is on the stage will be in your shot. What's outside will not.

4. LIBRARY: the tall, thin box on the right of your Flash document. Here you will find all your production elements (such as characters and props)—but only after you have created them!

5. TOOL BOX: on the left of your screen, the tall, thin window with pictures of pencils and brushes and arrows, etc. These are your tools for creating and manipulating artwork.

6. PROPERTY BOX: at the bottom of the screen; this is needed for changing line quality, adding tweens, etc.

7. PAGE LAYOUT: If something is missing from your screen, click WINDOW on your menu bar, find it and select it. Then it will pop up on your screen. If you have altered your document window and want to go back to Flash's default screen, click WINDOW on the menu bar, choose WORKSPACE LAYOUT from the sub menu, then DEFAULT from the ensuing sub-sub menu.

8. MAKE SURE YOU SAVE YOUR WORK ON A REGULAR BASIS or you will be sorry one day!!

SOME TOOLS:

Selection Tool: the black arrow. Use this when you want to select, grab, and move things. You can also alter artwork with it by grabbing the outside of an unselected graphic and dragging.

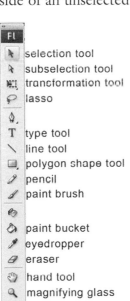

selection tool
subselection tool
transformation tool
lasso

T type tool
line tool
polygon shape tool
pencil
paint brush

paint bucket
eyedropper
eraser
hand tool
magnifying glass

line color

fill color

Subselection Tool: the white arrow. Click the edge of an unselected graphic with this tool and the graphic's outline becomes scattered with transformation points which you can use to pull and distort your image.

Transformation Tool: Use this on selected graphics and symbols to scale, skew, and rotate.

Onion Skin: This function lets you see more than one frame at a time so you can adjust animation sequentially, as if you were looking at drawings on top of each other on a light table. It will be explained in depth soon, but you switch it on with this icon:

PAINTING AND COLOR CHOOSING
(WITH AND WITHOUT OUTLINES)

Drawing and painting in Flash can be done with the following tools (note their icons in the tool box): Polygon Shape Tool, Pencil, Brush, Eraser.

There are two places to choose colors. Near the bottom of the tool box are smaller versions of the pencil and paint bucket icons. Below each is a square with a color in it. Clicking either square will bring up a color palette from which you can choose a color:

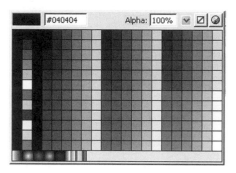

Your cursor will have turned into an eyedropper as well, with which you can click any artwork on your stage and choose a color.

Changing the color in the square below the pencil icon changes the color of your LINE. Changing the color in the square below the paint bucket icon changes the color of your FILL. If you don't want a line or a fill, choose the square with the red line through it.

If you want a GRADIENT FILL (where one color gradually changes to another), once you have opened the palette, click one of the gradient options at the bottom of the palette window.

There is also a COLOR WINDOW that opens by default in the upper right of your screen:

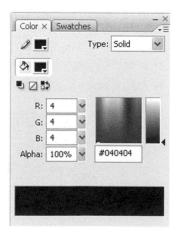

You can choose colors and gradients in this window too. This is also where you can alter the colors in your gradient.

Before you do the following exercises, create a folder on your desktop in which you will store all the elements you create for the projects and to which you will download pertinent files.

Exercise 1: DRAW A POLICE CAR

Doing this exercise will show you how to use the essential drawing tools in Flash. You can then apply the skills to your own ideas.

1. Select the RECTANGLE TOOL in the tool box.

2. In the PROPERTY BOX, change the stroke size of your line to 3. (To the right of the pencil icon is a square in which you can choose your color, just like the square in the tool box; to the right of this is a box with a number in it. Highlight this number and change it to 3.) Make sure your line color is black.

3. In the square under the paint bucket, choose a blue color. You may have figured out by now that you can change colors in the property box and color window as well. You may do so with impunity.

4. Click the rectangle tool on the stage, slightly above and left of center, then drag it down and to the right, creating a blue rectangle with a black border, like so:

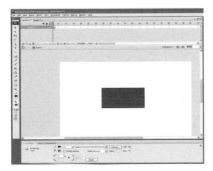

continued

5. Select the black arrow (aka the SELECTION TOOL). Notice that if you click the blue area of the rectangle and drag it, you separate the fill from the line:

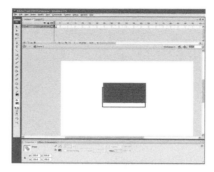

   Hit CTRL+Z to undo it. Notice if you click the lines you can likewise separate them from the fill:

   You want to do neither of these things. Undo as many times as necessary for you to get back to an unmolested rectangle.

6. Place the black arrow tool on the top line, near its center. Look carefully at the arrow and note that a little curve has appeared below it. If you do not see said curve, move the arrow until you do. If the tip of the arrow is on the line, it should appear.

7. When the curve appears, click the line and drag it slightly upward and to the right. Pretty cool, huh? You should have been able to deform the top of the rectangle so it looks like this:

continued

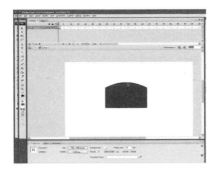

8. Similarly warp the front and back lines until you have a shape like this:

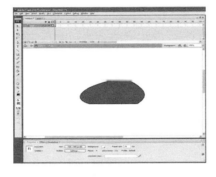

9. Making sure your shape is deselected (Shift+Control A or just click your mouse outside the shape), change the fill color to gray.

10. Use the rectangle tool to make a gray rectangle below the blue shape.

11. Use the black arrow tool to select the fill and line of the rectangle only. How? Click outside of it and drag a marquee around it, careful not to touch the blue shape.

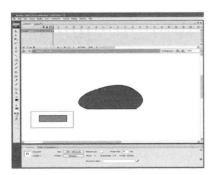

continued

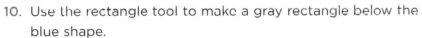

12. Grab your selected rectangle and drag it to the upper front of the blue shape.

13. Click outside of all the objects to deselect.

14. Much as you did in step 7, place the black arrow on the front line of the gray rectangle and warp it like it is below:

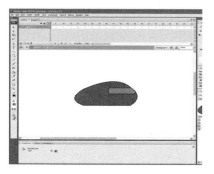

15. Click and hold down the rectangle tool icon in the tool box. A menu will drop down from which you should choose POLYSTAR TOOL. After doing so, go to the property box and click OPTIONS. A new window will open; where it says STYLE, change from polygon to STAR.

continued

Change the number of sides to six and change the Star Point Size to .70, then hit OK.

Change the fill color (the square next to the paint bucket icon) to yellow. Now drag the tool to an area outside of the art you've already created, and draw a star:

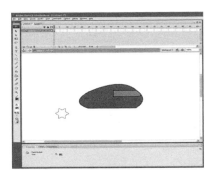

Using the black arrow, select the star, being careful not to select anything else. Drag the star and drop it roughly here on you art:

16. Choose the TYPE TOOL from the tool box (the big letter T). In the property box, choose arial black as your font, yellow as your color, and 25 as your size. Now click the type tool just to the right of the star and type the word "Po-lice" (the hyphen is important as it will give you street credibility). Click outside the art to deselect everything and you will have something like this:

continued

17. Choose the PAINT BRUSH TOOL. Near the bottom of the tool box are two circles—click the upper one. A menu of brush sizes will appear. Pick the third from the top. Change the fill color to black.

18. Paint this with the brush, in an area *outside* of all your art:

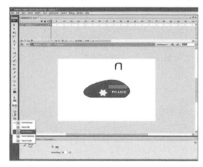

19. Change the fill color to red.

20. What you are going to do next is paint the inside of this red, but first you must close off the bottom. Right now the  paint brush is set to paint *over* existing lines, so first you must tell Flash you want to paint *under* the lines. To do this, click the icon just above the one which allowed you to change brush sizes, and choose PAINT BEHIND from the dropdown menu. Now paint a line across the bottom of the black-lined object you painted. As you paint, it appears you have painted over the black line, but once you finish and let go of the mouse button, Flash shows you that you in reality painted *under* the line. Yes, it would be nicer if you could see an accurate representation of what were painting while you were painting it, but that's just not how Flash rolls.

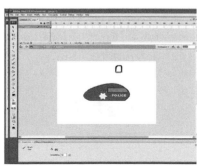

continued

21. Keeping the fill color red, choose the PAINT BUCKET TOOL, click in the white area of the object, and voilà, you have filled it with red.

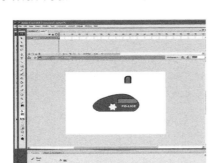

22. With the black arrow, select this entire object, then hit F8. A window will appear. In it, in the space for "name," type "light." For "type," choose "graphic." "Registration" is not important in this case, though we will deal with it later. Hit OK. Now you have turned your art into what Flash calls a SYMBOL. This means Flash now sees the lines and fill as one fused object and will always treat it like a unit.

23. Select the blue shape and all the type and shapes on it, and turn it into a symbol called "car."

24. Because your art has become symbols, if you click on any part of "light" or "car," you will have selected *all* of the object, not just fill or line. Grab "light" and drag it to the top of "car," like this. Depending on Flash's temperament,

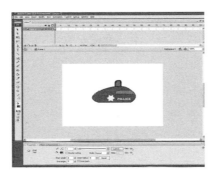

continued

it may be either behind or in front of "car." Keeping "light" selected, go to MODIFY in the menu bar, choose ARRANGE, then, if it is in front of "car," choose SEND TO BACK. (Choose BRING TO FRONT if it is in back.) Now that you know how to move a symbol front and back, make sure "light" is *behind* "car." Select "car" and "light" and make them a symbol called "car2." Remember, F8 converts art to a symbol.

25. In the tool box, your shape tool should still be set as the polystar tool. Click it and change it to OVAL TOOL.

26. Change the line color to NOTHING (square with red line through it). Change the fill color to black. Holding down the shift key, drag the oval tool until you have drawn a circle. (The shift key, by the way, makes the oval tool draw a perfect circle rather than an oval.)

27. Change the fill to gray and draw a smaller circle.

28. Select the gray circle with the black arrow and drag it into the middle of the black circle. If you have trouble position-ing it with the mouse, use the arrow keys on your key-board to finesse the placement.

29. Select both circles with the black arrow tool, then, using F8, turn it into a symbol called "wheel."

30. Drag "wheel" to the left bottom side of "car," then send it to the back (MODIFY ⟶ ARRANGE ⟶ SEND TO BACK).

31. Look in the LIBRARY. All your symbols are in there. Grab "wheel," drag it to the stage, line it up at the right bottom of the car, and send it to the back.

32. Select everything and convert it to a symbol called "finalcar."

continued

33. Click on "finalcar," choose the TRANFORM TOOL from the tool box and play with the following functions:

   A. Grab one of the corner points and watch how you can change the size. Holding down the shift key lets you scale proportionately.

   B. Click the points on the sides and pull. These let you change size in one direction only.

   C. If you place the cursor just outside one of the corners, the cursor becomes a semi-circle with an arrowhead. When the cursor looks like this, you can press the mouse button to ROTATE your art.

   D. Place your cursor just outside one of the lines and it turns into this:

   When it is shaped like that, you can press the mouse button and SKEW the artwork.

   E. Play with these tools, but when you're done, put the car back to its normal position and shape.

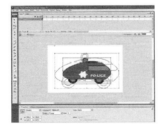

34. DON'T FORGET TO SAVE CONSTANTLY AS YOU WORK!!! Save this document as "Police Car."

So. Not to use the Lord's name in vain, but Jesus Christ, that was a lot of steps to just draw a police car! But once you are familiar with Flash, much of that process will be intuitive and you'll be able to build much better things faster.

Notice you used many different tools to make the car; this was for demonstration purposes. You could have used only

continued

the brush tool if you wanted to, but now you've been exposed to many methods, all equally valid.

MOTION TWEENS

1. In the *same document* in which you created the police car, notice in the TIMELINE that the first frame has a dot in it. That means it is a KEYFRAME. This is the frame on which you will start your TWEEN.

(What is a KEYFRAME? It is a frame in which your artwork changes somehow. Except, of course, for the *first* keyframe— nothing changes here because nothing pre-exists it.

What is a TWEEN? When you place a symbol at different parts of the stage on different frames, Flash will make the symbol move from one spot to the next over the amount of frames you chose. Unclear? Do the exercise and you'll get it.)

2. Using the transform tool, shrink the police car. Then drag it to the left of the screen.

3. Select the final frame (choose a frame number higher than the first frame; for example, if frame 1 is your first frame, you can choose frame 22 as your final frame). To select a frame, use the selection tool (the black arrow), then click the frame you want with the left mouse button. MAKE SURE YOU SELECT THE FRAME AND NOT ABOVE IT. The frame will turn black if you have selected it.

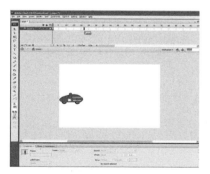

4. Convert to KEYFRAME (F6).

5. Select the final keyframe.

6. Place your symbol where you want the motion to end.

continued

7. Select both keyframes and all the frames in between. (You can do this by left-clicking on the first frame, then shift-left-clicking on the final frame. DO NOT drag the mouse with the button clicked!)

8. In the property box, in the TWEEN window, select MOTION.

9. Note that an arrow appears across the frames you selected.

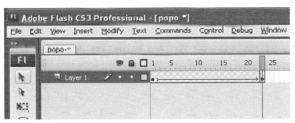

To Play This Back

Select the first frame, then hit ENTER. Your symbol should now move smoothly across the frame.

MOTION PATHS

1. Follow the first seven steps of MOTION TWEENING above.

2. Select the layer in which your motion tween exists.

3. Below the timeline, on the left side, to the right of the "insert layer" option is the "add motion guide" option. Click on it.

continued

4. A MOTION GUIDE LAYER will appear above your layer.

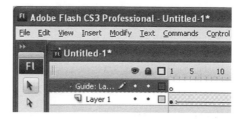

5. Select the layer (click on its name and all the frames will be selected). Make sure all the frames in the guide level are selected (i.e., they are black).

6. From the tool box, choose the PENCIL TOOL (a black stroke color is preferable but not necessary).

7. With the pencil, draw a motion path across the stage. It can be zigzags or loops, but should not be so cluttered as to confuse Flash.

8. Select the first keyframe of the motion tween.

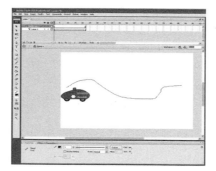

9. Using the SELECTION TOOL, select your symbol. There should be a small circle in the center. Grab the symbol from this circle, then drag the symbol until the circle is directly over the *start* of your motion path. You should feel the symbol snap to the start of the path.

continued

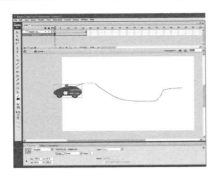

10. Select the last keyframe of the motion tween.

11. Using the selection tool, select your symbol. Grabbing the small circle in the center, drag the symbol until the circle is directly over the *end* of your motion path. Again, you should feel the symbol snap into place.

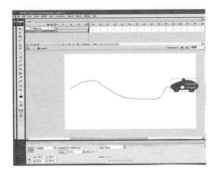

To Play This Back

Select the first frame, then hit enter. Your symbol should now happily follow the motion path you drew.

SHAPE TWEENS

Open a NEW DOCUMENT for this exercise. You will not need the police car for this one.

1. Start on frame 1, where a keyframe already exists.

2. In this frame, on the stage, create your shape. (I recommend that you make a shape with NO OUTLINE, as Flash will tween the outline separately from the fill and you might not like the look.)

continued

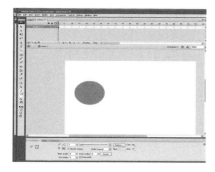

3. Next, select frame 22 in the timeline. Right-click it and make it a keyframe.

4. In this frame, alter your shape however you wish (using the selection tool, free transform tool, changing color, etc.).

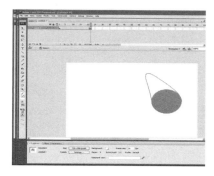

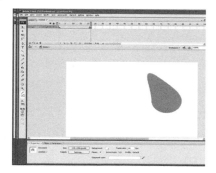

5. Select both keyframes and all the frames in between. (Do this by left-clicking on the first frame, then shift left-clicking on the final frame. DO NOT drag the mouse with the button clicked!)

6. In the "property" box, in the TWEEN window, select SHAPE.

continued

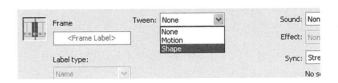

To Play This Back

Select the first frame, then hit enter.

If you want to make these tweens more elaborate, add keyframes between the main keyframes and change the position, size, and/or shape of the symbol/shape on these keyframes.

Problems? Did you select the frame in the correct layer? Did you click on the timeline and not on a layer? Did you have more than one frame selected when you created a keyframe, thereby making *many* keyframes?

If you had any problems, do the exercises again and pay close attention to the directions—follow them exactly and it will work!

Exercise 2: Car Skidding

For this exercise you will need the "finalcar" symbol you made previously, so I hope to hell you didn't throw it away.

1. Create a new document, making sure it is 24 frames per second.

2. Open the "Police Car" document.

3. In the library, select "finalcar," then hit CTRL +C (to COPY "finalcar").

4. Go back to your new document. (You can switch between open Flash documents by clicking the tabs at the upper left of you work area.)

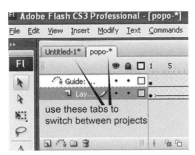

continued

5. Once in the new document, press CTRL+V (to PASTE "finalcar").

6. Shrink "finalcar" (using the TRANSFORM TOOL) and place it stage left like so:

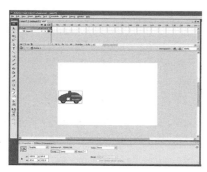

7. On frame 15, make a keyframe (F6). Move "finalcar" to the right side of the stage, and SKEW it backwards. Skewing is accomplished via the transform tool. With the cursor just above the top, drag the mouse left until "finalcar" looks like this:

8. Select frame 20 and convert to keyframe (F6).

9. Move "finalcar" to the right a little and skew it the opposite way.

10. Convert frame 26 to a keyframe and UNSKEW "finalcar" (i.e., straighten it out).

11. Select frame 45 and hit F6.

continued

12. Select all frames (they will all be black if selected), then, in the property box, choose MOTION TWEEN.

13. Go to www.guerrillaanimationbook.com and download "skid.mp3" to your desktop folder.

14. Create a new layer. The simplest way is to press the icon near the top left of the workspace.

15. Grab it and drag it below the preexisting layer.

16. It is now named "Layer 2." Double-click the name and then type in a new name: SOUND.

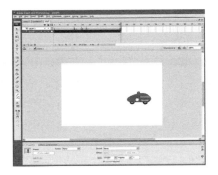

17. FILE → IMPORT → IMPORT TO LIBRARY. Via the window that pops up, navigate to your desktop folder, to which you should have saved "skid.mp3." Highlight "skid.mp3" and click OPEN.

18. With the SOUND layer selected in the timeline, grab "skid.mp3" from the library, drag it to the stage and drop it. It will appear as a waveform in the SOUND layer of the timeline.

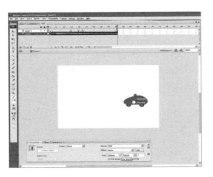

continued

19. Select the SOUND layer, then look at the property box. In the window marked "sound," "skid" should be visible. If not, use the arrow next to the window to select it. Then, in the "sync" window, choose "stream." This is the best setting to have sound at because it allows you to scroll through the soundtrack and analyze it frame by frame (which is good when you want to read a dialogue track).

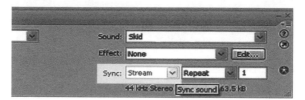

20. Select frame 1 and hit enter to play back.

Notice the change in shape as the car skids to a stop? It slants backwards, then it settles by slanting forward, then back again. This DISTORTION can be applied in many instances with motion. Even a character will lean and settle the same way when coming to a fast stop.

WALK EXERCISES

FLASH WALK (part 1)

Before doing the next two exercises, go to www.guerrilla animationbook.com and download the following:

moneyes.jpg

monhands.jpg

monstercln.jpg

Uarm.jpg

Larm.jpg

legcycle.fla

These next lessons will show you how to create complex characters whose parts you can adjust and adapt to different situations. You will end up creating a complete scene and, by modifying the lessons, you will be able to make television-quality animation.

continued

Take your time with these. Do them a couple of times, until all the nuances sink in. They contain many tools for your future use.

1. Create a new Flash document and save it as "walk."

2. Make sure it is 24 fps.

3. Create five new layers (so you have a total of six; one already existed when you created the file).

4. Name the top layer EYES, the next layer HAND, the next LARM (for "lower arm"), next UARM ("upper arm"), next BODY, next LEGS.

    Select frame 20 on all layers, click F5. (This converts everything from 1 to 20 into frames. Until you do this, Flash believes that nothing exists beyond frame 1.)

5. Select frame 1 of the EYES layer.

6. FILE → IMPORT → IMPORT TO STAGE.

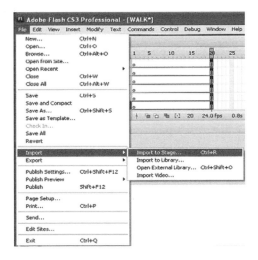

Find "moneyes.jpg" and click OK.

continued

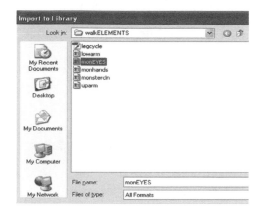

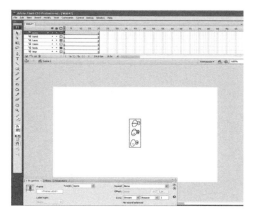

7. MODIFY → BITMAP → TRACE BITMAP. "Trace Bitmap" is Flash-speak for "vectorize." You have just taken raster art (i.e., art made of pixels) and converted it to vector art.

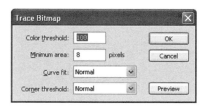

8. DESELECT the artwork (by clicking an area outside it). The raster art you imported was surrounded by a white border, which you must now delete. To do so, take the selection tool (black arrow) and select the area just outside of the eyes. All the useless whiteness should have been selected.

    Hit BACKSPACE to delete it.

continued

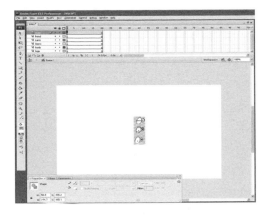

9. Pick colors and paint the eyes. (The lids should be the *same* color in all the eyes. The insides should be the same in all the eyes as well.) To paint, use the brush with paint-behind function and the paint bucket tool.

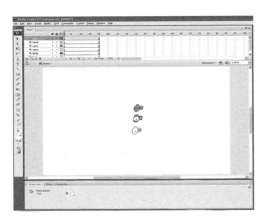

10. CONVERT TO SYMBOL. Select all, then hit F8. Call the symbol "eyes." Make sure you save it as a "graphic symbol," which will be the case with all symbols you create with this book.

Lock the EYES layer and turn off the visibility. This is so you don't accidentally edit the eyes while working on

continued

the next layer. You can leave it visible and unlocked if you wish, but my way is safer.

11. Select frame 1 of the HAND layer.

12. CTRL+R (this is another way to import to stage), choose "monhands.jpg."

13. Repeat step 8.

14. Paint the hand. Close off the open area with the paint brush (with your fill color), fill the rest with the paint bucket. Convert to a symbol called "hand," but before you hit OK, IT IS IMPORTANT THAT YOU SET THE REGISTRATION. Many times, it doesn't matter where the registration point of the symbol is. But in this exercise it will often matter. See how next to the word "registration" there is a grid with eight little white squares and one little black square? Choose a white square, click it, and it becomes the black square. The black square represents the PIVOT POINT of your artwork. The hand is going to pivot at the wrist, so if you choose the TOP MIDDLE SQUARE as the registration point, that will be the de facto JOINT from where the hand will move.

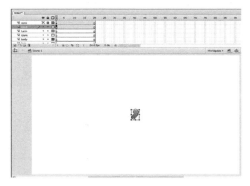

Lock the layer and turn off the visibility if you wish.

continued

15. Select frame 1 of the LARM layer. Import "Larm.jpg" to stage. Trace bitmap. Paint it the same color as the hand, then delete the white areas. If you need to, use the magnifying glass tool to zoom in while painting. To zoom back out, hold the ALT key down while using the glass. Convert to symbol called "Larm." MAKE SURE REGISTRATION IS WHERE IT IS INDICATED BELOW:

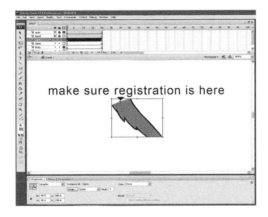

To do this, select the symbol and choose the TRANSFORM tool. Move the cursor to the white dot in the center, click on it and drag it to the desired spot. Use this method any time you wish to change registration points.

16. Select frame 1 of the UARM layer. Import "Uarm.jpg" to the stage. Trace bitmap. Paint it the same color as the hand, then delete the white areas. Convert to a symbol called "Uarm." Using the transform tool, place the registration point as shown here:

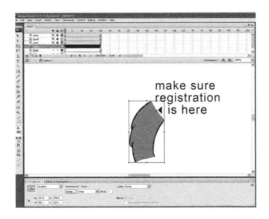

continued

17. On the BODY layer, import "monstercln.jpg" to the stage. Convert to bitmap, remove white, paint same color as hand, convert to symbol called "body." Registration can be in the center.

18. Find and open the Flash project called "legs" (you imported it from the web). In the library of "legs," select and copy the symbol called "legcycle."

19. Close "legs," return to "walk." Right-click on frame 1 of the LEGS layer and paste (CTRL+V). The leg cycle should now be in this layer.

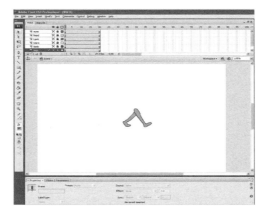

INTERMISSION

I don't know about you, but I need a break right about now. Get up, stretch, go for a walk, put a brick through someone's window. Then, thus refreshed, come back for . . .

FLASH WALK (Part 2)

1. Unlock each layer and make them visible. On the stage, line all your elements up so your monster looks like a

continued

monster. Note: the eyes will be stacked at this point—line up the bottom eyes with the monster's face like this:

2. On the EYES layer, animate a blink so that the eyes are shut on the down pose of the leg cycle. Here's how:

   A. MAKE SURE OTHER LAYERS ARE LOCKED.

   B. Turn on ONION SKIN. If you don't remember how, look at the picture below:

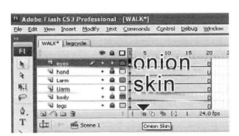

Once it's on, you will notice two handles on either side of the timeline cursor. You can grab these to expand and contract the amount of frames on either side of the cursor the Onion Skin function lets you see.

continued

C. Select frame 1 of the EYES layer.

D. Double-click the EYE symbol. This breaks it apart and allows you to edit it. Be careful, because every part is active now.

E. Select the CLOSED and HALF-OPEN EYES only, and move them away from the monster.

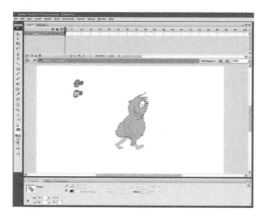

F. Select frame 12 (of the EYES layer). This is the second DOWN POSE of the cycle. Insert a keyframe (F6). Delete all the eyes on this frame only.

G. Go back to frame 1, select the closed eyes and hit CTRL+X.

H. Go to frame 12, hit CTRL+V, and place the eyes according to where the Onion Skin lets you see the open eyes.

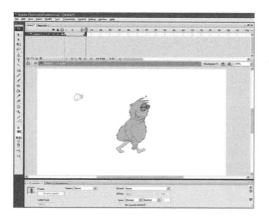

I. Insert a keyframe on frame 10 and move the HALF-CLOSED EYES onto the monster's face.

continued

J. Go to frame 1 and delete the HALF-CLOSED EYES.

K. Return to frame 10, hit CTRL+V and place the eyes.

L. Right-click frame 10, choose COPY FRAMES.

M. Right-click frame 18, choose PASTE FRAMES.

N. Right-click frame 1, choose COPY FRAMES.

O. Right-click frame 20, choose PASTE FRAMES.

P. At the top of the timeline, on the left of the screen and just to the right of the word "timeline" is a small blue arrow. Click this and you will return to the scene.

3. Turn off the visibility of the LARM and HAND layers. Lock all layers but UARM.

4. On the UARM layer, animate the upper arm moving. To do this:

A. Select frame 1 of UARM layer.

B. Place the UARM symbol like this (note: the first frame of the leg cycle is the CONTACT POSE):

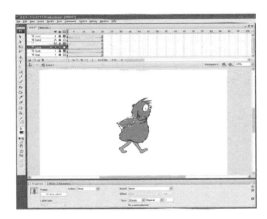

C. Make a keyframe at the next contact pose (frame 11).

D. Using the transform tool, rotate UARM forward so that it has swung forward.

E. Right-click frame 1, choose COPY FRAMES.

F. Right-click frame 21, choose PASTE FRAMES.

G. Select all frames in this layer; make a motion tween.

continued

Flash   127

H. Convert frame 20 into a keyframe.

I. REMOVE frame 21 (shift + F5).

Why did we create frame 21 only to delete it? It's so Flash could create a motion tween that returned to frame 1, with frame 20 perfectly positioned to lead back to 1 (since the arm movement is a cycle). Frame 21 stands in for frame 1 while the tween is created, then after converting 20 to a keyframe, we eliminate 21.

J. Lock this layer.

5. Unlock LARM layer and animate it. The lower arm should move faster than and independently of the upper arm; when all the way back it should be stretched out and when all the way forward it should be tucked in.

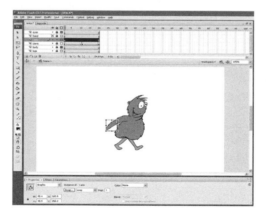

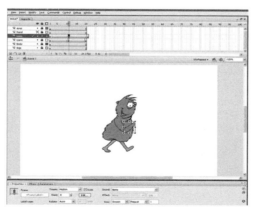

A. On frame 1, place LARM at the bottom of UARM.

B. Make a keyframe on frame 11.

continued

C. Rotate LARM so it has swung forward and tucked.

D. Right-click frame 1, choose COPY FRAMES.

E. Right-click frame 21, choose PASTE FRAMES.

F. Select all frames in this layer; make a motion tween.

G. Convert frame 20 into a keyframe.

H. Remove frame 21 (shift + F5).

I. Hit enter to play it back. Notice that the lower arm moves away from the upper arm. To remedy this, select all the odd numbered frames in the layer and convert them to keyframes (F6). On each of these new keyframes, move the lower arm so that it meets up with the upper arm properly. Once the movement looks nice to you, lock the layer.

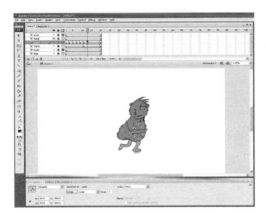

6. We will do something similar with the hand now, but with a special focus on creating OVERLAPPING ACTION. How? When the arm has gone forward and is on its first frame of motion back, keep the hand moving forward for that one frame. Do the same on the reverse action. Use frames 1 and 11 as your extremes (with 21 being a copy of 1). Make 1 look like this:

continued

And make 11 look like this:

Select all the frames, add a motion tween, convert frame 20 to a keyframe, and remove frame 21. Then select all the odd-numbered frames, convert them to keyframes, and adjust the hand in each so that it is properly hinged to the arm.

7. Once the hand and both arm elements move well together, make them into a symbol:

A. Make sure all three layers are unlocked.

B. Select all frames in all three layers.

C. COPY FRAMES (remember, you can't just copy, it must be COPY FRAMES).

D. INSERT ⟶ NEW SYMBOL. Name the symbol "arm."

E. Right-click frame 1, PASTE FRAMES.

F. Hit the BACK ARROW (blue arrow) to return to the scene.

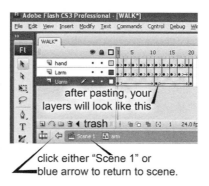

after pasting, your layers will look like this

click either "Scene 1" or blue arrow to return to scene.

G. DELETE the UARM, LARM, and HAND layers (select them and drag them to the trash).

H. Create a new layer called ARM1.

I. Select frame 1 of this layer and place the "arm" symbol there.

continued

8. In the library, double click on the "arm" symbol. This opens it up so you can edit it.

9. Select all the frames.

10. Copy all the frames (remember: COPY FRAMES, not just copy).

11. Hit the back arrow (blue arrow) at the top of the timeline.

12. INSERT ⟶ NEW SYMBOL.

   A. Name this symbol "Arm2."

   B. Make sure registration is at shoulder.

   C. Right-click frame 1 and PASTE FRAMES.

   D. Rearrange the frames so that the arm moves with an action that is the exact opposite of ARM1. To do this, do the following in each layer:

      i. Select frames 1–11.

      ii Cut frames.

      iii. Select frame 21.

      iv. Paste frames in frame 21.

      v. Convert frame 30 to keyframe.

      vi. Remove frame 31 (right-click, REMOVE FRAMES).

      vii. Remove frames 1–10.

   E. When finished, hit the back arrow (blue arrow) to return to the scene.

   F. Insert new layer.

   G. Call it ARM2.

   H. Place it BEHIND all other layers.

   I. Select frame 1.

   J. Place ARM2 on the stage in a position appropriate to the action.

13. Select frame 1 and hit enter. Is your animation looking good? Is it 20 frames long? Why not? It should be.

14. SAVE YOUR DOCUMENT.

15. SAVE YOUR DOCUMENT AS "MONSTER."

continued

16. Combine the EYES layer, ARM layer, and BODY layer (*but not ARM2*) into a new symbol. To do this:

    A. Select all frames in these layers.

    B. Copy frames.

    C. INSERT ⟶ NEW SYMBOL.

    D. Name symbol "upper."

    E. Right-click frame 1, PASTE FRAMES.

    F. EXIT the symbol (back arrow).

17. Create a new layer called UPPER. Make it the top layer. Select frame 1 of this layer.

18. Drag the "upper" symbol from the library onto the stage and place it exactly where the body is.

19. Hit enter to make sure it moves right.

20. If it looks good, delete your EYES, BODY, and ARM layers.

21. Your monster should be made of three layers now: UPPER on the top, LEGS in the middle, and ARM2 on the bottom.

22. Lock the LEGS layer.

23. On the UPPER and ARM2 layers, create keyframes (F6) on the DOWN POSES and UP POSES.

24. Right-click frame 1 on the UPPER layer, copy frames, right-click frame 21, paste frames.

25. Right-click frame 1 on the ARM2 layer, copy frames, right-click frame 21, paste frames.

26. Select the first DOWN POSE KEYFRAME (frame 6) on the UPPER and ARM2 layers. (Click frame 6 of UPPER, then shift-click frame 6 of ARM2; frame 6 of LEGS will be selected too, but since you locked it, no changes can be made to it.)

27. Choose the FREE TRANSFORM TOOL.

28. With the free transform tool, give the selected layers a SQUASH. Remember, you want to maintain the character's volume, so, don't just make it shorter, make it fatter as well. Compare the before and after pictures below:

continued

normal ▾   squashed ▾

29. Give a squash to the next DOWN FRAME; make sure the UPPER and ARM2 layers are highlighted and you've selected all elements (CTRL+A).

30. Make a keyframe on frame 10 for the UPPER and ARM2 layers (this is the UP POSE).

31. Select frame 10 of UPPER and ARM2.

32. With the free transform tool, give the selected layers a stretch (again, maintain volume by making it thinner as well as taller):

normal ▾   stretched ▾

33. Give a stretch to the next up pose (UPPER and ARM2 layers, all elements).

34. Select all frames in the UPPER layer and give it a motion tween, then do the same for the ARM2 layer.

35. On both layers, convert frame 20 to a keyframe.

36. Delete frame 21 on both layers.

37. SAVE.

38. Under "control" in the menu bar, choose "loop playback," then hit enter to watch.

INTERMISSION #2

Okay, time to stretch again, and maybe even own up to breaking that window. Take five minutes, then return for:

continued

FLASH WALK (Part 3):

1. Open a new Flash document. Make sure it is 24 frames per second. Now, using what you have learned, create a background, one that has a floor and a wall roughly proportioned like this:

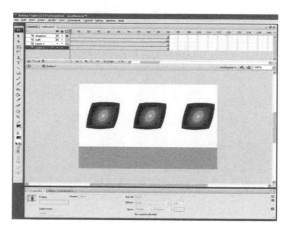

   You can decorate as you wish or copy mine.

2. Save as "walk scene."

3. Open your "monster walk" document.

4. Create a symbol called "monster" that contains all the monster elements for the 20 frames.

5. In the library, copy the "monster" symbol.

6. Go back to your new document ("walk scene").

7. Paste the "monster" symbol in the library.

8. Create a new MONSTER layer and drag the "monster" symbol just to the left of the stage like in the next illustration.

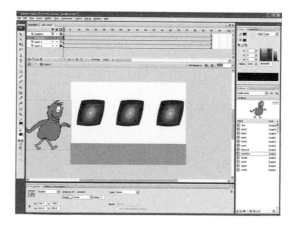

continued

9. Make a keyframe on frame 90 of the MONSTER layer.

10. Place the "monster" symbol on the right side of the screen, just outside the stage. Though there are only 20 frames of animation inside the symbol, it will repeat and play for the duration of the scene.

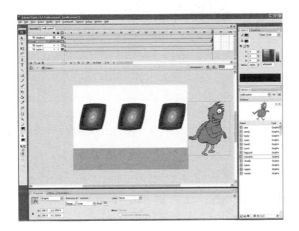

11. Select all frames in this layer.

12. Make a motion tween on this layer.

13. Play with the timing (if you want) by either changing the position of the character in the final keyframe or by changing the frame number that the final keyframe is on.

14. Celebrate International Anarchy Day by throwing your monitor through a plate-glass window. Especially if you're at school.

15. Run before the pigs arrive.

Take one more break here, then return for a quick postscript.

ONE MORE LESSON:

1. Make a new layer called SHADOW and make sure it is at the top of all the layers.

2. Draw this shape in black on the layer (use whatever method you want: brush, polygon tool, etc):

continued

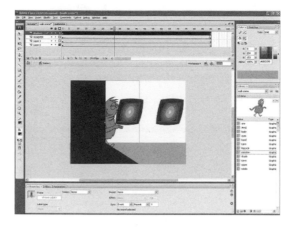

3. When finished, turn it into a symbol called "shadow."

4. Using the black arrow, click on the shadow on the stage.

5. In the "property" box, find the window labeled "color" and click the arrow next to it. A list of options will be revealed and you will pick "alpha." For whatever reason, the makers of Flash chose the word "alpha" to mean "opacity." In this instance, alpha has nothing to do with alpha channels.

6. When you do this, a new window will open just to the right of the color window. This window says 100%. Using the arrow next to it, change the percentage to 27:

7. Hit enter and your monster will walk through the scene, emerging from the shadows as he does.

You can make an animated TV show with the techniques learned in this chapter; just change them to fit your project.

continued

OUTPUTTING

Now that you have finished your animation, what do you do with it? Well, there are several answers.

1. If you are making a movie for the web, you can export your animation as either an SWF file, a QuickTime movie, or an AVI. I recommend outputting as a QuickTime. SWFs—which are Flash movies—are unreliable and the picture sometimes plays at a different speed from the sound.

    Your QuickTime movie should be small in pixel dimensions (360 pixels wide for anything over a minute). You might want to compress the QuickTime later with a compression program. An excellent program for compression is Sorenson Squeeze.

    Here's what you do: Under "file" in the menu bar, choose "export," then "export movie":

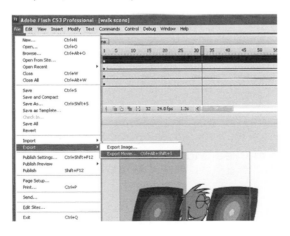

continued

At the bottom of the window that opens, there is a small box marked "Save as type." In it you choose "Quick-Time (*.mov)." You also use this window to choose where you will save the movie and what you will call it. Having done all that, hit SAVE:

A new window will appear, in which you set your pixel dimensions. You can leave all the other options alone. If, however, you wish to alter how your movie is compressed, click on "QuickTime Settings" in the lower left of the window.

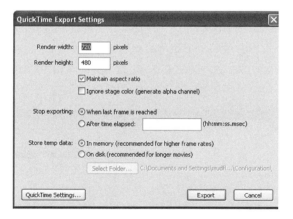

Yet another window will appear, at the top of which is a section marked "video":

continued

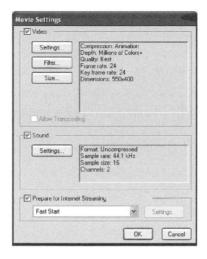

Click the "settings" button below the word "video," and another window will appear. At the top there is a little box marked COMPRESSION TYPE. In here you can choose different types of compression. It will probably be set on "Animation" compression by default, which is fine.

In the window's lower left there is a fader with which you can adjust the level of compression quality. To increase the compression (i.e., make the file smaller), DECREASE the quality:

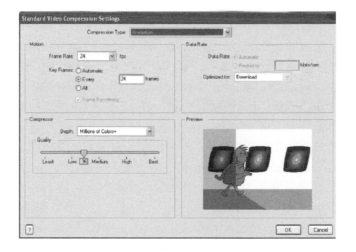

After choosing your settings, hit OK, then OK on the previous window, then EXPORT on the first window you opened. Flash will now make your movie.

continued

2. If you are making a project that will go on television, you should export a QuickTime movie that is the proper size for the type of broadcast it is intended for. If you are creating for standard (North American Teleivision), your film should be 720 pixels wide. If you are creating for HDTV, the pixel dimensions should be either 1280 x 720 or 1920 x 1080.

   If you are creating something professionally for TV, ask your client for the specs on what size to make it. In this instance, you should make sure there is NO compression on your QuickTime.

   Also, when working for TV, you will either animate at 30 frames per second, or, more likely, have to convert your 24 fps animation to 30 fps. This process is called a "3:2 pulldown," and I will show you how to do it in the After Effects chapter.

3. If you are making animation (of characters only, with no background) to use in After Effects, you would most likely export it as PNG sequence. A PNG sequence is a series of still images with alpha channels. The alpha channel means that when your animation is exported, the characters will have no background around them and you can place them over any new background with impunity. Many people, by the way, refer to PNGs as "pings."

   Let's do this as an exercise now. Open your "monster-walk" project and save it as "WALKexp." Grab the shadow and background layers and drag them to the little trash can icon in the timeline. Only your character animation should exist in the document now.

   Now do this: FILE ⟶ EXPORT ⟶ EXPORT MOVIE. In the window that appears, choose where you are out-putting to, then, at the bottom in the "Save as type" box, choose "PNG sequence."

   Create or choose a folder to export to. It is best to save to a folder dedicated only to these PNGs, as there will be ninety of them.

continued

In the box above the "Save as type" box, change the file name to "monwalk." Your PNG sequence will be numbered like this: monwalk0001.png, monwalk0002.png, etc. Hit SAVE. A window will appear where you can set the size of the output. If you've been working at 720 x 480, it will default to this. Hit OK.

Now, save this project, then save as "WALKexp2." Select the MONSTER layer, then remove the motion tween from it so that the monster now is walking in place rather than across the screen. Place the monster in the center of the stage. Then export this as a PNG sequence with the file name "moncycle."

DON'T LOSE THESE SEQUENCES because you will use them in your After Effects tutorials.

When will that be? Turn the page . . .

CHAPTER 14

After Effects

Adobe After Effects is an amazing program that facilitates animation production in many ways. There is so much you can do with this program that I won't be able to come close to showing it all to you. But I will show you how you can use it to composite a simple scene, a more complex scene in 3D space, and how to use it to cheat. Once you know that, you can figure out wilder stuff. At the very least, you will be able to put together professional-looking scenes.

WORKSPACE

When you open Adobe After Effects, the workspace will look something like this:

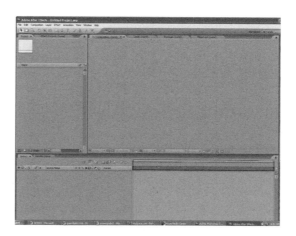

Step one with any project is to create a new composition. You do that by clicking on "composition" in the menu bar and choosing "new composition":

When you do so, another window will open in which you will set up your project's length, frame rate, and aspect ratio. You can give the composition a name if you so desire; naming your comp (that's slang for "composition," in case you want to be one of the cool kids) is important when doing very complex things involving multiple compositions and pre-comps, but for now, don't worry about it. Also for now, work at 24 frames per second, though there will be times you might want to work at 30 or 29.97 fps.

Now take a look around at the workspace. If you don't have it open on your computer, look at the first illustration in this chapter. At the top is a menu bar. Below that is a tool bar.

Then below that, in the left corner, is the project box, behind which is tucked the effects control box.

To the right is a very important space—your composition window. This is where your movie will be visible. Below this is the timeline, where you will arrange all the elements in your film.

What follows is a series of exercises that will show you how to use all the functions necessary to make a film.

EXERCISE #1

Before starting this exercise, create a folder on your hard drive called "AEtutorials." Then, go to www.guerrillaanimationbook.com and download "elements.psd" to this folder. Keep all elements from this project in the same folder. Then:

continued

1. Open After Effects

2. COMPOSITION ⟶ NEW COMPOSITION

Set width to 720, Height to 480

Frame rate: 24 fps

Duration 0:00:10:00

Hit OK.

3. FILE ⟶ IMPORT ⟶ MULTIPLE FILES (or command+alt+I).

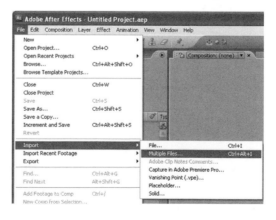

continued

A. Look in the "AEtutorial" folder.

B. Select "elements.psd" and hit OPEN (or double-click).

A new box opens. "Import Kind" should be set to "Footage." Under "Layer Options," select "choose layer." Select "fence."

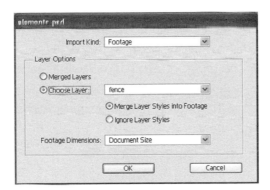

C. Repeat B for "light," "lamp" and "ground."

D. Go to the folder in which you saved your "monwalk" PNGs from the Flash chapter. Select it and hit OPEN (or double click it). Select the first file in the folder ("monwalk_0001.png"). Make sure the box in the lower left marked "PNG Sequence" is checked.
    Click OPEN.

continued

E. Find and select the folder in which you saved your moncycle PNGs and open it.

Select first file in folder ("moncycle0001").

Make sure the box in the lower left marked "PNG Sequence" is checked.

Click OPEN.

If you are particularly observant, you will have noticed that these elements have appeared in the project window in the upper left of the screen. Both "monwalk" and "moncycle," though made up of many PNGs, appear as single elements. After Effects sees them as a self-contained animated sequence that cannot be violated:

continued

4. Once they are so arranged, Click DONE.

5. Drag these elements into the left-hand side of the timeline (as shown in the illustration). Rearrange them so that "fence" is the topmost, then "light," "lamp," "monwalk," "moncycle," and "ground." You must first deselect them (CTRL+D), then select each individually to do this:

6. On the screen (the composition window) you should see all the elements. Many of the elements are too big:

We shall remedy that shortly.

7. Notice that there is a triangular arrow next to the FENCE layer in the timeline window (actually, there's an arrow next to all the layers, but, like the rainforests, we don't really care about them right now). Click this arrow and the word "transform" will appear below it, accompanied by another arrow.

Click this new arrow and be amazed at all the options that unfold below it:

continued

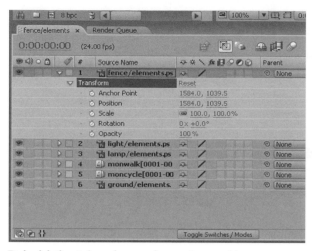

Behold the triangles and ensuing options . . .

For now you are only concerned with the option called SCALE. Next to the word "scale" are two 100% numbers. Highlight one, type in "27," then hit enter. Both numbers will change because they are linked (if you ever want to unlink them, click the little chain-link icon beside them):

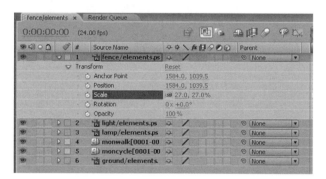

8. Highlight "light" *and* "lamp" in the timeline, then click the triangle beside one. Note both layers opened up.

9. Making sure both are still highlighted, click the triangle beside "transform" on the LIGHT layer.

10. Change SCALE to 21%. Notice both the light and lamp levels changed scale.

11. Making sure both layers are still highlighted, grab the images in the composition area with the cursor and drag them to the left of the stage until the straight left edge of the LIGHT layer is flush left with the screen.

continued

12. Click all the triangles you opened to close them and neaten up the timeline. From now on, when you're finished with an open layer, close the triangle.

13. Change the scale of the GROUND layer to 27%.

14. Click the triangle next to "monwalk," then open TRANSFORM.

15. Change the scale from 100% to 57%. You can't see him because in the animation you output from Flash, he hasn't as yet entered the frame. But if you move the current time indicator to anywhere past five frames, you will see him:

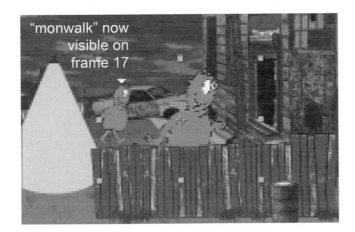

"monwalk" now visible on frame 17

continued

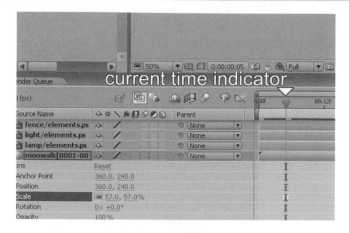

current time indicator

16. Bring the current time indicator back to zero. Drag "mon-walk" left and up, placing him under the light. The marquee around him should be flush left with the screen, like so:

The small squares near the edge of the highlighted area are the "marquee." The highlight has been added to help point out the marquee—you will not have one on your screen.

Again, you won't see the monster in the first frame since he starts his walk off-screen.

17. On the MONCYCLE layer, change the scale from 100% to 74%.

18. Remember to click the open triangle to close the layer you opened.

19. In the timeline window, all the way to the left, are eye icons. Click the one next to MONCYCLE. That layer should vanish from sight.

continued

20. Select "light," open it up, open the transform option.

21. Change OPACITY from 100% to 37%. By the way, you can either highlight the number and type in a new one or place the cursor on the number, click it and, holding the mouse button down, drag the mouse either left or right to change the value.

22. Drag the "Current Time Indicator" to the right until you see the Monster walk into the frame. If he is not in an aesthetically pleasing place, move him to one BUT ONLY UP OR DOWN, NOT LEFT OR RIGHT. In my project, on frame 20, I moved him down to here and I like it that way:

Moncycle repositioned down a little, seen through semi-translucent light.

23. Select "light" again, and choose EFFECT → BLUR & SHARPEN → FAST BLUR.

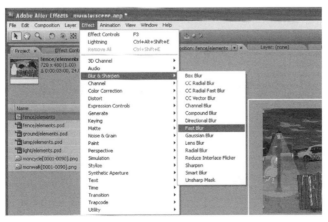

continued

24. Over your "project" box is now an "effects control" box. Find the word "blurriness" and adjust the value to 57.

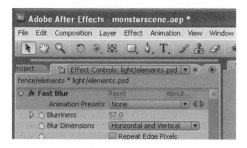

Now your light has a soft glow. Click the project tab next to the effects control tab (at the top of the box) to display the project box again. Use these tabs to go back and forth between Project and Effects Controls:

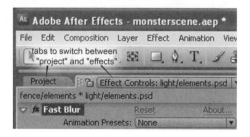

25. WORK AREA

When you created your composition, you made it ten seconds long. That is much longer than your animation. So, do this:

At the top of the timeline you will notice a gray bar with blue handles. This is called your WORK AREA. Right now it spans the length of the timeline. Grab the blue handle on the right and drag it left until it is flush with where the monwalk animation ends:

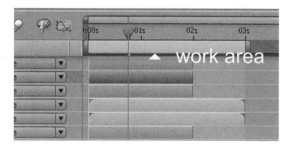

continued

Why did you do that? Because soon you will PREVIEW your movie, and since After Effects previews whatever you have selected as your work area, this helps us avoid watching a whole lot of nothing.

26. Click the eye icon next to the MONCYCLE layer to make it visible again. Select the layer then go to EFFECTS ⟶ COLOR CORRECTION ⟶ HUE/SATURATION:

The "Effects Control" window will reappear. In it, grab the MASTER HUE knob and turn it until your Monster has turned pink:

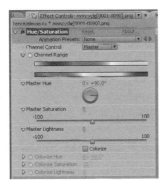

27. Look at the next illustration. Grab the "Current Time Indicator" and move it back and forth over the timeline—notice the animation move.

Marvel at how your monster walks from left to right.

continued

Your project is small now, so "scrubbing" like this is easy. As your film becomes more and more complex, scrubbing will become more difficult, perhaps enough so that it infuriates you. Cool.

28. While "monwalk" is a progressive walk, "moncycle" is a WALK CYCLE and must be moved across the screen over time. So . . .

29. Open the layer and then open TRANSFORM

30. Making sure the timeline cursor is at 0, click on the clock icon to the left of POSITION.

Here you should become aware of another tool. At the bottom of the timeline is a tiny fader. This lets you expand and contract the size of the timeline. If you need to see the timeline at a frame-by-frame level, drag the cursor to the right. To see more of it (but at larger increments), pull the fader left. While doing the next bit you might find it nice to change at what size you view the timeline:

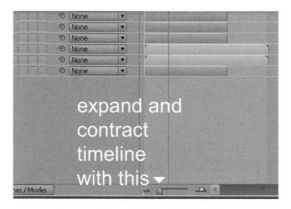

expand and contract timeline with this ▼

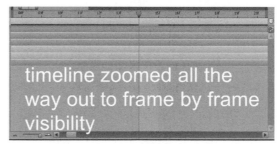

timeline zoomed all the way out to frame by frame visibility

31. Now move the current time indicator to the right so it is flush with the work area/end of the "monwalk" animation.

continued

32. Drag the "moncycle" animation all the way to the right of the screen until the character is off-screen.

33. Hit 0 on the number keypad to watch. If you are using a laptop which has no number keypad, go to COMPOSITION → PREVIEW → RAM PREVIEW.

34. To finesse the scene a bit:

    A. Select GROUND, choose EFFECT → BLUR & SHARPEN → FAST BLUR.

    B. Make the blur 10.

    C. Give FENCE a FAST BLUR of 5.

    D. Give MONCYCLE a FAST BLUR of 5.

    E. With MONCYCLE still selected, go to EFFECTS → COLOR CORRECTION → BRIGHTNESS & CONTRAST.

    F. Change brightness to -50.

    G. Change brightness of FENCE to -31.

    H. Change brightness of GROUND to -10.

35. One more thing: sound. Return to www.guerrillaanimation book.com and download "song.mp3." Then import it into your After Effects project, drag it to your timeline (I find it best to keep my sound layers at the bottom of the timeline), then HIT 0 on the number keypad to play back.

    Based on this exercise, you can now begin constructing simple scenes in After Effects. However, proceed to the next exercise to learn more detailed tricks.

POTENTIAL PITFALL

Did your scene suddenly disappear? Make sure you haven't accidentally left the comp—usually if your scene vanishes, clicking here brings you back:

continued

EXERCISE #2

For some of you, Exercise #1 will be sufficient to make the movies you want. With just that little bit of knowledge you will be able to construct many types of scenes.

But this next exercise represents a quantum leap in what you can do.

1. Go to www.guerrillaanimationbook.com and download the following files:

   AEsky.jpg   AEtree01.jpg

   AEtree02.jpg   boid.mov

2. Start a new After Effects project with a new composition that has the same settings as the last one (24 fps, 720 x 480, ten seconds duration).

3. Import the following elements into your project:

   AEsky.jpg   AEtree01.jpg

   AEtree02.jpg   boid.mov

   Put AEsky.jpg on the bottom, AEtree01.jpg above that, then the boid.mov next, and finally AEtree02.jpg.

4. Here is the new, quantum leaping, mind-blowing step: you will put your elements into 3D space.

   A. Look at the illustration—the highlighted area on the timeline shows a tiny cube with boxes to click below it. Click these boxes in your project for the TREES and BOID levels (but not the SKY level). You have made them 3D levels:

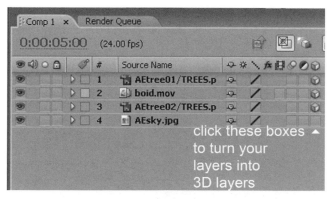

click these boxes to turn your layers into 3D layers

continued

B. Click the triangular arrow next to each layer, then the triangular arrow next to "transform" once the levels have opened up. Allow me to explain the numbers to the right of the word "position." These are X, Y, and Z coordinates to define where in 3D space your artwork will exist. If you click the cube icon again (deselecting it), the last number (the Z) will vanish.

C. For the AEtree02 layer, change the Z number from 0.0 to 700.0:

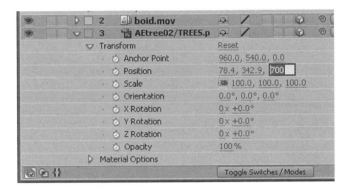

What the hell? The trees just *shrunk*! Actually, that's a good thing. With the arrow tool, click somewhere on the trees to grab them and drag them so their bottoms are at the bottom of the screen, centered like so:

AEtrees02.jpg lined up at the bottom of the frame.

D. For the BOID layer, change the Z coordinate to 250. What you have just done is tell After Effects that

continued

the bird is closer to the camera than the AEtree02 layer. Also, change the scale of the bird to 30%.

E. Select AEtrees01, grab them and drag them from their position in the last illustration to here:

We won't change the Z coordinate; this layer will be closest to the camera.

F. Open the BOID layer. Make sure the current time indicator is on frame 0. Click the clock icon next to "position," then drag the bird to the left like so:

Now move the time indicator to eight seconds, and drag the bird off-screen to the right, like this:

continued

G. Make the right side of the work area flush with the end of the bird animation:

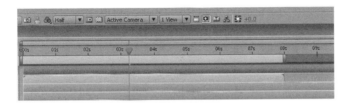

H. In the menu bar there is a heading called "layer." Click on it and choose NEW, then CAMERA:

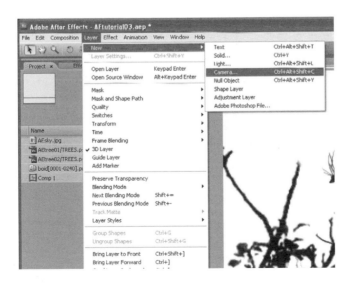

continued

A big, complicated-looking box will pop up. Just hit okay. I have done countless projects in After Effects and have never made any adjustments to this window:

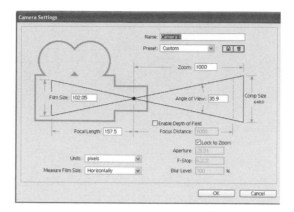

I. Open the camera layer, then open "transform" (using the little triangles). Click the clock next to "position" (make sure current time indicator is at frame 0).

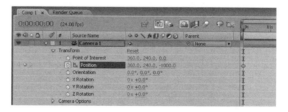

J. Drag the time indicator to eight seconds and change the Z coordinate of "position" to -500.

K. On the number keypad on your keyboard, hit 0 to watch the movie. (Or: COMPOSITION ⟶ PREVIEW ⟶ RAM PREVIEW).

Note the following:

1. The SKY layer was not put on a separate 3D layer and was not affected by the camera moves. This gives the illusion that it, like the actual sky in the real world, is very far away.

2. The SKY layer was twice the size of the final picture. Why? So when the camera moved around, the sky would not get cut off. It's like a bleed area in printing.

3. The trees.psd layer was likewise longer than the screen size to accommodate the camera move.

4. If you want to finesse this scene, experiment with adding varying amounts of fast blur to each layer.

EXERCISE #3

1. Open After Effects project #2 and save it as "AEtutorial03."

2. At the bottom of your composition window, click the little box labeled "1 View" and change it to "2 Views Horizontal":

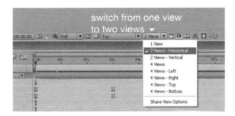

Now you have two views of your scene. Look and see which view is selected at the moment. You can tell because it will have yellow triangles in each of its four corners:

continued

3. Click on the view next to it and watch that side get triangles in the corners while the first view loses them.

4. Make sure the left-hand view is selected. In another box at the bottom of the composition window there is a box that has a percentage in it, most likely 100%. Change it to 12.5%.

Notice that the screen on the left shrunk. That's because that was the side you had selected.

5. Select the right-hand side (by clicking on it) and shrink that to 50% (in the same box where you changed the left-hand value).

6. In the timeline, select your camera level. An upside-down red triangle appears in the left-hand screen:

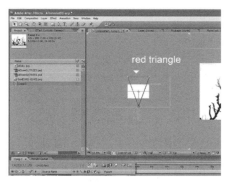

At the bottom of it, if you look closely, are arrows which allow you to move your camera through 3D space. If you want to see these arrows up close, change the view size from 12.5% to 200%, then, using the hand tool, move the camera into view:

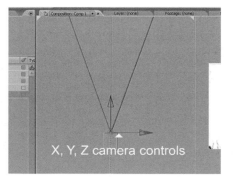

continued

But before touching these . . .

7. Click on the left-hand screen to select it.

8. Bring the timeline indicator to frame 0, then click the clock next to the word "position." You have just eliminated your previous camera move. Now click the clock again. You are now set to create a new camera move. ALSO CLICK THE CLOCK NEXT TO "POINT OF INTEREST."

9. In the timeline, move the current time indicator to three seconds.

10. On the left-hand screen, after making sure it is still selected, bring your cursor over the little arrows at the bottom of the red triangle. Without clicking the button, move the mouse around and you will notice the letters X, Y, and Z appear next to the arrow. When the X is next to the arrow, you can click the mouse and move the camera along the X axis. When the Y appears, you can click and move along the Y axis. Likewise with the Z. So, at the three-second mark, move a little to the left on the X axis, centering the bird in the frame.

11. Move the current time indicator to six seconds and move the camera along the X axis to the right until you find the bird. Then move in along the Z axis and up a little on the Y.

12. Move the current time indicator to eight seconds and move the camera along the X axis until you find the bird again.

13. Play back.

14. In the camera level in the timeline, shift-click all the keyframes (gray diamonds) in the position row. They should all be yellow diamonds now. That means they are selected.

15. Right-click on any of these diamonds. A menu should appear, from which you choose "Keyframe Interpolation":

continued

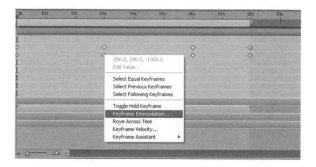

16. This invokes another window, in which you adjust "Temporal Interpolation" and "Spatial Interpolation" to "Continuous Bezier," then hit OK:

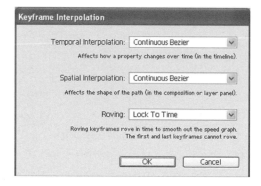

Notice in the left-hand view that your camera move is now along an arc. Play it back.

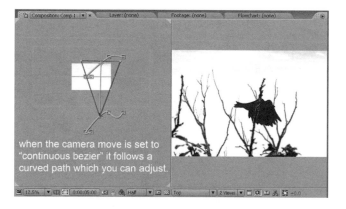

when the camera move is set to "continuous bezier" it follows a curved path which you can adjust.

17. Along these arcs, at the keyframes, are handles with which you can make the arcs more arc-y, if you so desire.

continued

control handles

18. If the sudden acceleration at keyframe 2 bothers you, grab keyframe 2 in the lower arc (indicated in the illustration) and move it so as to smooth out the curve. You can also move keyframe 2 (in both the point of interest and position levels) closer to keyframe 3. There are many ways to adjust and finesse your move.

Do these exercises a couple of times verbatim, then start making your own versions of them, substituting your own backgrounds and animation. Soon you will be able to apply and adapt all the concepts to brand new, original works of your own. And won't that be cool?

PUPPET PINS

The latest version of After Effects includes a new feature called Puppet Pins that allows you to add joints to a drawing, making it moveable. It essentially allows you to create a bone structure in a drawing and then animate it.

Allow me to demonstrate. I have created a simple character:

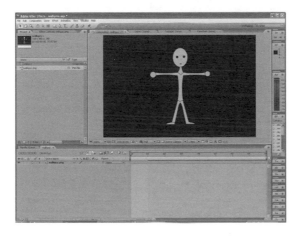

After choosing the Puppet Pin tool (either by pressing CTRL+P or clicking this icon):

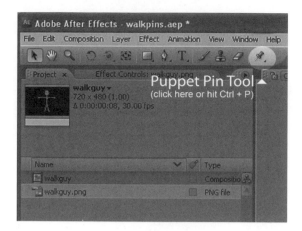

I simply place pins where I want to create joints, by clicking the mouse in the desired spots:

In the timeline, notice that in the character's layer there is now a heading called EFFECTS, under which is a heading called PUPPET, under which is yet another heading called MESH 1:

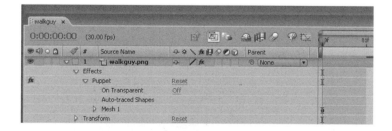

When I open the MESH 1 heading, I am confronted with an option called DEFORM. After opening this, I find separate headings for each of the Puppet Pins I created:

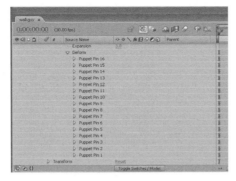

You don't necessarily have to use these controls, but they are there to micromanage your animation if you wish.

Next, I move the current time indicator to frame 5 (a completely arbitrary choice). Here I move some of the joints to animate the character:

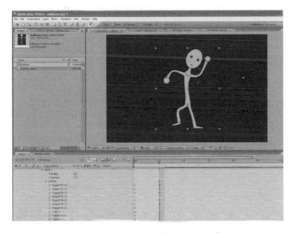

I hit the 0 key on the number pad to watch a preview, and I miraculously have an animated character. After Effects inbetweened the movement between the two positions for me.

Here is an example of an initial pose, an anticipation, and a jump using this method:

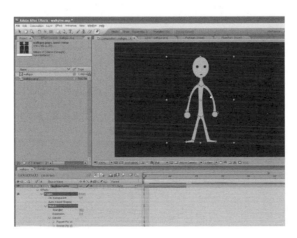

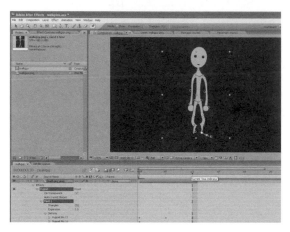

Of course, these are very simple examples. If you want to do more complex things, you will most likely need to break your character into layers. In this next example, I will show you why.

Since the arms are drawn into the body of this new character, when I use the pins to move it, the whole character warps:

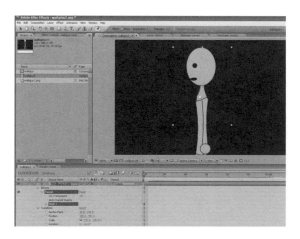

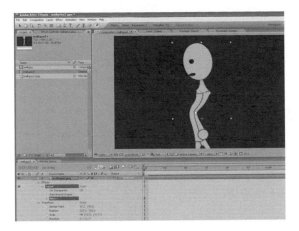

With the arm as its own layer, however, it moves fine:

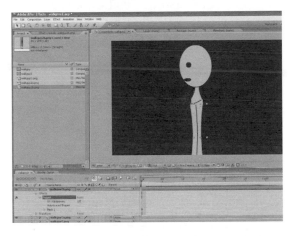

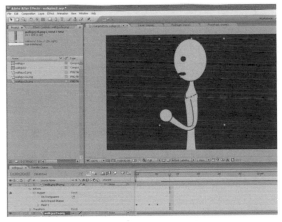

Other 2D software has similar functions as well. For example, Anime Studio Pro lets you build characters with a bone rigging, and a company called Trick or Script has created a plug-in for Flash that lets you give your characters bones (see Appendix).

Such animation is similar to 3D computer animation in that the character is built with a certain skeletal structure, which you then manipulate to create movement. Becoming familiar with these 2D aspects will help you if you want to move into 3D animation.

OUTPUTTING

Generally you will output your work under two distinct circumstances. The first is when you are making your own work under your own terms. In this situation, your output size and dimensions will be entirely up to you. If you need your file to be small, output at a small pixel dimension and add compression. If you need high resolution, don't compress, and output at whatever size your final destination is.

The second circumstance is when you are creating work for a client, in which case you must output at whatever size and format the client requests. You might be asked to do a QuickTime, a Cineon sequence, or something more esoteric. Luckily, After Effects can output in every professional format.

But what about converting to 30 frames per second from 24? You know, like I mentioned in the Flash chapter?

Well, here the client or editor will give you more information, but, just for fun, let's output one of your exercises and I'll show you how to make a simple QuickTime and point out how to convert frame rates at the same time.

Open one of the three previous exercises. Click on the composition window, then, in the menu bar, click on COMPOSITION → MAKE MOVIE:

This should cause the "render queue" window to open. In most cases, it will open up over your timeline. If it does, it will look like this, and there will be tabs in the upper left with which you can switch back and forth to the timeline.

In the "render queue" window, there are three elements with which you need to be concerned: RENDER SETTINGS, OUTPUT, MODULE, and OUTPUT TO:

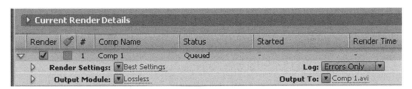

One note: sometimes the render queue does not come up immediately when you use the MAKE MOVE-command. First a box asking you to save as an AVI or a MOV appears. If you say OK to this, then you will get the queue. If you have trouble getting the render queue, then go under "window" in the menu bar and in the dropdown menu you will find "render queue."

Next to the words "Render Settings" are either the words "Best Settings" or "Current Settings." Your first mission is to click these words. A new window will appear:

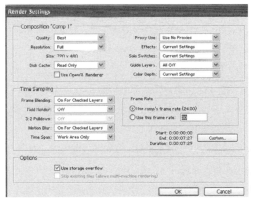

In the upper left, there is a window marked "quality." If you are making a high-resolution movie, make sure this is set on BEST. If not, you can choose DRAFT.

Below "quality" is "resolution." For high resolution, choose FULL. To shrink your movie, choose HALF, THIRD, or QUARTER. Notice that choosing different resolutions changes the size number below.

In the middle right, where it says "frame rate," make sure the setting is 24.

CONVERTING FROM 24 FRAMES PER SECOND TO 30

In the middle left are some options marked "time sampling." If you want to convert your animation from 24 fps to 30, this is where you do it. In the boxes marked "field render" and "3:2 pulldown," you will find several options. *Usually* in field render you choose UPPER FIELD FIRST and in 3:2 pulldown you choose WSSWW (you must select something in field render before you can select anything in the 3:2 pulldown box):

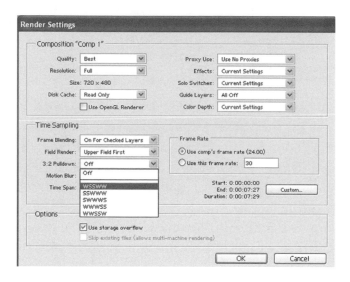

However, if your converted animation has lines running through some of the frames, try switching to LOWER FIELD FIRST and SSWWW. Some combination will work.

Below all this crap is another box called "time span." This is where you decide how long your movie will be, that is, whether it will be the entire length of your composition, the length of your work area, or some custom length you have chosen.

By default, WORK AREA ONLY will be selected. If you recall, the work area is defined by the bar above your timeline, the bar with blue handles. Therefore, with this option selected, you will output the area between the blue handles.

With LENGTH OF COMP selected, your entire composition will be made into a movie.

If you choose CUSTOM, a small window will materialize in which you can define the frames on which your movie will start and end.

Regardless, having satisfied all the above, hit OK. Next, you will want to click the "Lossless" next to OUTPUT MODULE.

Near the top of the window that materializes, there is a little box labeled "format," and it is here you choose whether you will output a QuickTime movie, video for windows, or one of a number of other sublime and bizarre options:

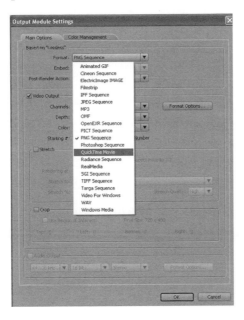

A few options below this is a box marked "channels." If you are outputting something around which you want to have an alpha channel, change the option in the "channels" box to "RGB + Alpha." Otherwise, don't touch it. I mean it:

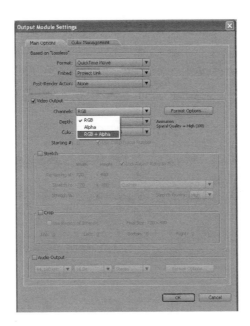

To the right of the channels box is a button labeled "format options." Clicking this gives you another window called "compression settings." Among the many options is NONE. This is what you choose if your project is high resolution. Otherwise, use either ANIMATION or SORENSON 3 if you have those options:

There is a fader near the bottom of this window which lets you increase the compression by decreasing quality. Use this option if it makes you happy. When you're finished, hit OK.

You are now back at the "output module settings" window, at the bottom of which you should see an AUDIO OUTPUT option. Switch this on if your project has sound. Even if you are compressing your file, you can leave the audio settings as they are (which is high quality). Hit OK.

Finally, in the render queue, to the right of the words "output to" will be the name of your movie. After Effects will have named it after your composition, so, if you didn't name your composition, your movie will be called "comp.mov" at this point.

Click the movie's name and a window will open in which you can give it a new title if you desire. In this same window you also choose where to save the movie.

Hit SAVE when you are done then hit RENDER in the render queue and wait for your movie to be made (the time this takes depends on how long and complex your movie is as well as how fast your computer can work.)

TONES AND HIGHLIGHTS—A BIG CHEAT

So what the hell are tones and highlights anyway? They are shades of light and shadow placed on an animated 2D character to give the character some depth. Tones and highlights are most often used in modern animation as a way to offset otherwise crappy animation and design. Most of what's considered "classic" animation DOES NOT use tones and highlights.

Bugs Bunny rarely has them, neither does Tom or Jerry. On the rare occasions they do have tones and highlights, it's motivated by an extreme light source or because they are in deep shadows.

And here's what these celebrated tones and highlights look like:

tones and highlights

painted flat

And this is how they are made. After an animator finishes his or her drawings for a scene, another artist takes those drawings, and, on a separate piece of paper, draws shaded areas that will become the tone and highlight. All these layers are then scanned into the computer and colored. Then the tones and highlights are made translucent and placed above the character before all the layers are composited together.

Don't worry if you didn't follow that—I'm going to show you a much simpler way to do it.

Open up the first After Effects project you did, the one with the monster animation. Choose the layer with the "moncycle" animation in it. In the menu bar, click on LAYER ⟶ LAYER STYLES ⟶ BEVEL AND EMBOSS:

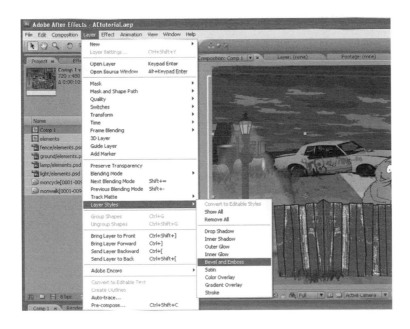

In your timeline, bevel and emboss options will appear:

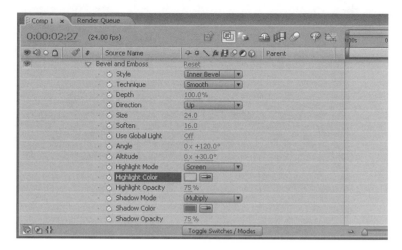

Change the size to 24, soften to 16 (I chose these numbers because I felt they looked good; feel free to choose your own). Then change the highlight color to a light pink and the shadow to a dark pink, and boo-yaa, you're finished. Play it back and marvel at your skills:

CHAPTER 15

Work Habits

We all have our own style of working, but over the years I have found certain ways to use time efficiently, wisely, and impressively (i.e., others are impressed that I never miss a deadline). Allow me to share some of these here.

STRETCH

When you spend long hours hunched over a drawing table or in front of a computer, your back and neck will get tight and painful, leading to chronic backaches and headaches. Try to remember to get up at least once an hour and stretch. Do whatever kind of stretching exercise you like, but the point is, GET UP OUT OF THE HUNCHED POSITION AT LEAST ONCE AN HOUR!!!

You will probably forget to do this every hour (I do), but make it your goal. And when other people laugh at you for doing it, just remember, when they're in traction at the hospital, *you* can laugh at *them*!

SAVE

Save your work as often as possible when working on the computer. I save constantly, several times an hour. If it hasn't happened to you yet, you will one day know that sick feeling most of us have felt when the computer freezes and you haven't saved in three hours and all that work is GONE FOREVER!!

That doesn't happen to me anymore because I save all the time. In fact, it's such a habit of mine that when I am drawing on paper, I find my left thumb and forefinger automatically pressing a phantom CTRL+S key on my drawing table every five minutes or so.

ACT IT OUT/USE A MIRROR/VIDEO REFERENCE

When figuring out animation, don't be afraid to get up and act out the move to see how it's done. If you have a character who is going to punch someone, get up and pretend to throw a punch. See how you stand in your anticipation pose, during the punch, and how you follow through. Do you settle subtly or violently?

Keep a small mirror with you when you work so you can reference facial gestures and mouth shapes. Mirrors are very helpful when animating dialogue.

And, if you can, videotape yourself or someone else doing moves you want to animate. Video reference can help you understand complex motion. In the cheat chapter I talked about printing rotos of existing animation to copy from. You can do the same with your video reference, giving you frame-by-frame paper images of the action.

This is not cheating, by the way—using mirrors and filmed reference are old techniques. Rotoscoping—that is, tracing over live-action film—was patented in 1917. When a technique has been around that long, it isn't cheating anymore.

DRAW THE SCENE YOU REALLY WANT TO DO FIRST

When embarking on a film, I usually have a scene that I really want to animate, more than any other scene in the film. For years, however, I would never do that scene first, opting instead to animate the film in order.

After a while I realized that I was often impatient and sloppy with the scenes leading up to the one I was itching to do. I now know it's best to work on the bits I have passion for first, then move on to other sections. What usually happens is by the time I finish that first scene I will have built up a passion for another, to which I then move.

Follow your desire and the quality of your work will be higher.

BACK UP YOUR FILES

While in the midst of a hectic project with a tight deadline, I don't like to stop and back up all my work to another drive or to DVDs. If there's a lull in the action, I want to go to sleep. And if there's no lull, I don't want to break my momentum.

However, it's good to back everything up after each day's work. That way, if your hard drive fries, you will only be one day behind schedule. It's rare that something will happen to wipe out your computer, but it does happen. It's happened to me a few times, and I have lost some things forever. And it didn't make me happy. I'm *still* not happy about it.

Also, when I finish a project, I try to make two backups of it and store them in different buildings. I use my house for one and another studio for the other. This decreases the chances of a catastrophe obliterating my work off of the face of the earth. I figure if both buildings are destroyed, then something so terrible will be going on, my stupid project will no longer be very important.

APPROACH A PROJECT SLOWLY AND CALMLY

When starting a new project, I often feel compelled to immediately start animating and putting things together without planning it out first. But over the course of many jobs I have learned that it's better to start slowly and carefully.

For example, instead of animating from my first basic storyboard, it's often better to add several character poses to the board in order to decide how the animation will play out. It's good to make layouts, and make them detailed if you have the time. I used to feel guilty spending the first few days of a project making inspirational sketches, reviewing reference material, and brainstorming ideas. I felt a vague sort of panic that made me want to start doing final animation right away.

But it turns out that taking a couple of days to really sort out the direction of a project is A GOOD THING. It's just like driving somewhere unfamiliar—take a minute to study the map first, don't just get in the car and start driving!

BEWARE CONSISTENT LONG HOURS

Long hours are part of the world of animation, especially as an outsider. In 1997 I made a short film called *Attack of the Hungry Hungry Nipples.* It was financed by Manga Entertainment/Palm Pictures and I agreed to finish it in two months. The film was four minutes long, and so those two months were ample time, provided that I worked every day and slept very little.

I got into the following routine: I would wake between 9 and 10 a.m. and immediately begin working. With very brief breaks for meals, etc., I would work until 5 a.m., at which time I would go to sleep.

Working through the night and sleeping during the day I found was a good combination, because by 10 a.m. my neighborhood had gotten so noisy, I couldn't sleep anymore. I *had* to get up. It was bright outside, the phone would start ringing—the momentum of the daytime world would sweep me up and back to work. Oversleeping was not an option; it was impossible.

Now, this is not a schedule you want to maintain over a lifetime. It's fairly unhealthy, and nowadays I make sure to put time to exercise in there. Animation is a very sedentary profession, and so we animators must learn to get out and about so as to prevent our muscles from atrophying.

And remember, REAL LIFE is important too. Stay in touch with your friends, and don't forget to have fun. Grueling work is part of guerrilla filmmaking because we enjoy the work. But keep some balance as well.

KEEP YOUR WORKSPACE NICE

Whatever you can do to make the area in which you work pleasant, do it. Try to have room to move around, places to store things, somewhere to shove clutter quickly when it becomes overwhelming, and make sure your desk and computer are at heights that allow you to work relatively painlessly.

NEVER THROW ANYTHING OUT

When I'm on a project, I never throw out any artwork or memo or note. The items I feel are no longer important go into a folder I label "crap," but they do not get destroyed until the project is completely finished. I have had too many moments when I've found myself needing something I threw away the previous week. With a "crap" file, everything exists until you are completely done.

TRY THE EASY WAY FIRST

Any time you wonder whether you should approach a situation via an easy method vs. a difficult one, try the simple approach first. If it works, cool! You didn't waste your time with the more involved way. And if it doesn't work, you didn't waste too much time before using the difficult approach.

CHAPTER 16

Motivation/Inspiration

Why make a film to begin with? It's laborious and there's a very good chance only five people besides your friends and family will see it.

The key lies in remembering to stay in touch with the creative spark that made you want to do the film in the first place, the spark you can barely remember when you're inundated with repetitive work.

If you dedicate yourself to making worthwhile, quality films, you will never fail. You may never sell anything, but you will not have failed.

Don't be discouraged by mistakes you make. Don't be afraid to redo animation if you don't like it. Don't be afraid to throw out an entire scene if it's not working. That doesn't mean you're no good, it merely means you are on the path to perfection.

In the next section I will relate stories of how I kept forging ahead after being rejected in some way, only to find later that the rejection had opened a door to success.

I will tell you stories that should help strengthen the platitudes put forth in this chapter. Just remember: BELIEVE IN YOURSELF!!!

PART II

ANECDOTAL SECTION

Introduction to the Anecdotal Section

The next several chapters tell how I managed to carve out a career for myself as an animation director. These stories from twenty years of trying and succeeding (as well as failing) in the animation business will strengthen some of the technical lessons from Part One, as well as impart new lessons of a more philosophical and inspirational nature.

We will learn to play well with others, to believe in ourselves, and to work hard (but not too hard), and we will try to integrate being a successful animator with being a successful human being.

If you are seeking to create animation professionally, especially in a less-than-mainstream fashion, I hope this section will be instructional, informative, and perhaps even inspiring.

There are many ways to enter the animation industry. Most people use the front door. Me, I burrowed my way in like a rat through a crack in the foundation. I've managed to stay, though people are always trying to smack me with a broom.

Upon my journey I learned these poignant lessons:

- The vicious cat who attacks you senselessly might actually be really funny if you think about it.
- Write down your dreams. Especially if they make you laugh so hard you wake up.
- Believe in yourself.
- Believe in yourself. (It's so important, it's a lesson TWICE!)
- Don't listen to the people who tell you not to believe in yourself.
- When you're successful, spread it around!!

- You never really know what's going to happen next, do you?
- There are 24 frames in every second of film.
- If you are picking someone up after school, you might miss the gangstas with the AKs, so plan ahead.
- You never know how long it will take for a seed to grow, so don't despair!!
- Many people will want you to be a failure because that makes them feel comfortable with their own lack of success. IGNORE THEM!!
- Don't sell anything away forever for less than one million dollars!!!
- You can bring things back to life, or try anyway, even when the answer is supposed to be no.
- If you are talented, be humble and gracious about it.
- Don't try to make a project serve too many needs if that means it loses its focus.
- If you're up for a job, WANT IT, and let 'em know you want it.
- When someone says a job is too difficult to do, that's an opportunity for you to step up and say "I can do it."
- Give the client what they ask for, even if you don't believe them.
- Be very careful when you work with people who don't understand animation.
- Act like a sucker and you will get treated like one.
- Hard work is okay, but Jesus, don't kill yourself!

In the next several chapters, I'll tell you how I learned them.

CHAPTER 17

Boston 1986: The Evil Cat Is Born

I was a film student at Boston University. I didn't buy into a lot of traditional film school theory. I believed (and still do) that movie productions are bloated and inefficient. I thought movies could be made better and more cheaply than they were. I felt that not enough attention was paid to having good scripts and acting, and that too much was paid to slickness and overpriced movie stars. I mean, was it *really* necessary to have two tractor-trailer trucks filled with lights to shoot one simple scene? Or to pay John Travolta $20 million *and* give him a jet?

I felt that *Rocky, Star Wars*, and *ET* had fatally infected mainstream American moviemaking with their formulaic, inane hokiness. I was adamant about this in most of my papers in school, and was usually alone in my opinions.

No matter. I believed in myself, and that was enough with which to square off against the world.

For my 16 mm production class, I was working with two friends, Tom and Joe Kane, who are two of the most talented, funniest people I have ever known. We were writing short, anarchic comedy bits that we planned to string together with some kind of unifying theme, not unlike *Monty Python's Flying Circus*. We were not concerned with "arcs" and "third act crises," or having the second act inciting action occur on page 62. We merely wanted to be funny.

So we wrote a fake commercial for an action figure who drinks too much, pukes on the hood of his Camaro, then gets into fights with the cops; a commercial for a gun magazine with a free swimsuit issue; an exposé seeking to find out who bones boneless chickens—clever stuff that was going to destroy all of Shakespeare's credibility as a writer.

MEETING JOSEPH MONTGOLFIER

The writing went well. We gathered props and costumes, rehearsed our roles, and began filming. And then we met Joseph Montgolfier.

Who, you might ask, is Joseph Montgolfier? And I'd answer, "Why, he's the man who invented the first hot air balloon. In France. About one hundred years before we met him."

At that time, WGBH, the local PBS station, was occasionally showing a short animated film (made with construction paper cut-outs) called "A Balloon Goes Up." It featured narration, in English but with a fake French accent, about how Mssr. Montgolfier invented the first hot air balloon. The film was quite absurd and we thought it was one of the funniest things we'd ever seen, though it wasn't *meant* to be funny. We vaguely decided to make a similar film as part of our epic.

MEETING ORVILLE

Orville was a badass. A *total* badass. He was a gray cat who belonged to a friend of the girl I was dating at the time.

I could never get the hang of Orville. I'd be sitting down and he would jump on my lap and purr and I'd pet him. Then, for no reason I could ever see, he would become filled with the Holy Spirit and attack the hell out of me, snarling and scratching and causing me to bleed. It was like having a Tasmanian Devil on my lap. A Tasmanian Devil on PCP.

I reached the point where I wouldn't go near Orville because I knew it would end in great misery for me.

Then one night I was dreaming. An evil gray cat that looked exactly like Orville was chasing me around an apartment. I'd run into a room, shut the door, turn around, and find he was waiting for me, ready to do some damage. So I'd run out of that room, shutting the door before he could get out, turn around, and see him staring at me menacingly again. Room after room, I could not escape this evil cat!

And my dream had a narrator who spoke in English with a fake French accent. The Narrator explained that this cat was very dangerous and "had just escaped from prison because he had previously blown up a duke, a duchess, and three Belgian businessmen with watches."

Well, what could I do upon hearing this line, this insanely nonsensical bit of fake French-accented narration in my dream? I began laughing so hard that I woke myself up. And I woke up my girlfriend, who, annoyed, mumbled in a drowsy state of anger, "What are you laughing about?"

So I told her, slowly and calmly so as not to bust out laughing again, that there was an evil cat who had just escaped from prison because he had previously blown up a duke, a duchess, and three Belgian businessmen with watches.

I guess that was the last thing she expected to hear, because she started laughing too.

The next morning I wrote the script for a little cartoon about a small boy and his evil pet cat called "Jean Jean and the Evil Cat," using much of my dream's narration.

Lesson: The vicious cat who attacks you senselessly might actually be really funny if you think about it.

Lesson: Write down your dreams. Especially if they make you laugh so hard you wake up.

I storyboarded the script and explained it to Tom and Joe, who thought it was funny. A few days later, on New Year's Eve, I stayed up all night making the artwork. (By the way, this is part of guerrilla filmmaking—you work while others party. Then you have a movie and they have empty bottles and a headache. . . .)

Like the art in the Joseph Montgolfier film, my art was all made from construction paper cut-outs, which is just as well because I didn't know how to draw then.

Three Belgian businessmen with watches.

A few months later, all the filming was done. Not just on the animation, but on about six or seven live-action bits as well. Though the animation seemed like just a minor part of the whole collection of films (to which we gave the title *Wrecked'm, Nearly Killed'm*), it would eventually give me an entire career.

In addition to making *Wrecked'm*, I had a full load of courses, a weekend job as a janitor, and an internship on a PBS show that was filming at WGBH. (Interestingly, though it's not relevant, Kevin Bacon and Kyra Sedgwick met while acting in this film, an *American Playhouse* production called *Lemon Sky*).*

But, despite my full schedule, by the middle of May of 1987, *Wrecked'm, Nearly Killed'm* was all cut together (back in the day we used actual film and actually cut it, actually). The sound was edited and mixed, the negative had been cut, and everything was in neat little boxes, properly labeled. It was ready to be turned into final screening prints. (For those of you familiar with only digital filmmaking, a PRINT is a final version of a movie, made from the cut negative. It contains sound, on what is called an "optical sound stripe," and is what gets run through the projector in theaters.)

The DuArt film lab in New York had a Boston office, and it was there that I took these elements so they could be shipped to New York and turned into film prints and videotapes. The people at the lab had by now gotten used to the strange title of the film and had stopped looking askance at me whenever I came in.

This is when a strange coincidence occurred.

MEETING GRAHAM CHAPMAN

Graham Chapman was one very important sixth of Monty Python,** who were the biggest influence on my filmmaking and sense of humor.*** The night I shipped the film off to be printed, I attended a

---

* Also interesting but not relevant: while on this film I met Bernadette from the kids show *Zoom* (she was the one who did the cool trick with her arms in the opening credits). When I met her she was an adult and working at WGBH. I said to her, "You're Bernadette from *Zoom*? Cool! Do the arm thing!" and she looked at me with extreme disgust and loathing and said, "No, I'm not going to do the arm thing." I didn't understand then how presumptuous and obnoxious it was for me to say that, but now I do. Sorry, Bernadette!

** You *do* know who Monty Python was, right?

*** Other influences, for the record: Woody Allen, Chuck Jones, Stanley Kubrick, the Marx Brothers, *The Young Ones*.

performance given by Mr. Chapman in Boston. It was very funny and I was honored to shake his hand afterwards.

Now, that may not *seem* like a strange coincidence, but read on and you'll see. . . .

CHAPTER 18

New York 1987: The Big Pond

Shortly thereafter I moved to New York and began working as a Parking PA (Production Assistant) on a low-budget feature film. What's a Parking PA? Well, it's like this: The production would set up in various neighborhoods and us Parking PAs had to stay up all night on the street telling people they couldn't park in front of their own buildings because movie vehicles would need the spots the next morning.

Naturally, we weren't very popular with the locals. We tried to impress them by saying "But it's a *movie*!" and they'd say, "Who's in it?" and we'd say "Ernest Borgnine," and they'd say, "Fuck that, I'm parking here. Bitch."

Back in those days, HBO, Cinemax, Showtime, etc., used to show short funny films to fill in the gaps between feature films. So, in my spare time, I tried to sell *Wrecked'm, Nearly Killed'm* either in its entirety or in parts to one of these major cable networks.

First, I sent query letters to all the networks, describing each short bit contained in the film. I almost didn't mention that "Jean Jean and the Evil Cat" was animated because it was so limited in its animation (and so crappy) that I thought that technically it might not even be animation. Lucky for me that I did mention it, however, or the film might never have gotten sold.

All the networks wrote back saying I needed to submit the film through a distributor. HBO/Cinemax was nice enough to include a list of some for me.

So I began bringing the film to distributors—that is, when I wasn't making people angry by telling them not to park in front of their own homes.

One afternoon, before heading off to the set, I got a phone call from the office of Charles Samu at HBO/Cinemax. They asked me to send the film directly to them instead of waiting for a distributor.

Why? I had no idea at the time, but Charles Samu, head of on-air promotions at HBO/Cinemax, was also a connoisseur of animation and constantly looking for new and unique animated films. If I hadn't mentioned that there was animation in *Wrecked'm*—if I had succumbed to my doubts that "Jean Jean and the Evil Cat" wasn't good enough to be called animation—Charles would not have asked to see the film, and would not have subsequently acquired the rights to put it on an upcoming Cinemax series hosted by . . . *Graham Chapman.*

And thus the coincidence. I met Graham Chapman the day I sent the film off to be printed, then a couple of months later the film was on a show he was hosting. I don't know about *you*, but *I* think that's pretty cool.

The first incarnation of the Evil Cat.

With any film or television deal, there is a good amount of negotiating. Even with my puny deal, this was the case. Since I was working as a Parking PA, I had to do most of my negotiating from payphones around Brooklyn and the Bronx, on the job. I'd be discussing the agreement with Charles and then have to excuse myself, cover the mouthpiece, and yell at someone, "Hey, I said you can't park there, we're making a movie! Yes, with that guy from *McHale's Navy*!" then go back to my business while hearing, in the background, "Fuck that, I'm parking here. Bitch."

Here's where I want to make a few comments I feel are perhaps the most useful to a filmmaker who is starting out. The biggest point is BELIEVE IN YOURSELF. Today, I don't like to show "Jean Jean and the Evil Cat" to anybody because the technical quality is so poor. But back then I believed in it. I had the guts to send it to HBO/Cinemax and I was rewarded. By conventional wisdom, I shouldn't have sent that film anywhere.

However, I was lucky to have a professor at BU, Robert Hooper, who was completely encouraging. When I outlined my plans to send the film to cable networks, he replied "Go for it. Send it everywhere." He could've said, "Well, the lighting isn't perfect," or "The sound is iffy in places," and discouraged me, but he saw that my enthusiasm, mixed with the fact that the film was genuinely funny, meant it had a shot. He taught me many things, but BELIEVE IN YOURSELF was the biggest and best lesson.

In my production classes the previous year, I had professors who told me I had to make projects with serious dramatic arcs and character development. Those are important things to learn, I suppose, but I wasn't *feeling* it. As a result, my work was lackluster that year. I made nothing I was proud of, nothing I felt I could sell, nothing I wanted to share with others.

But thankfully for my final production class I had a professor who allowed me to go with my instincts and strengths. As a result, I made something I could sell.

AND ON THE FLIPSIDE . . .

A related point (a corollary perhaps?) is, while you are believing in yourself, DON'T LISTEN TO THE PEOPLE WHO TELL YOU *NOT* TO BELIEVE IN YOURSELF.

When I told one of my former classmates I sold the film to Cinemax, he snickered, shook his head, and said with utter disbelief, "How'd you manage *that*?" His attitude was, "How did you, a mere piece of shit, sell a film to a major network when I, if I had only ever finished a film once in my life, really ought to be crowned Lord God Almighty?"

Other people insisted that I must be mistaken, that I must really mean my film was going to be on community access cable, certainly *not* Cinemax.

Others gave me advice about the money I got (which, I think, was $750, which, yes, is nothing really, but I didn't care—my film was on a major cable network, and in terms of starting a career, that was price-less), telling me "Oh they ripped you off. You need to renegotiate. You got reamed dude, that's crap money." Of course, none of those people had ever sold anything (and, as far as I know, still haven't).

If you take a risk and start climbing, others will try to drag you down. It makes them feel better about the fact that they haven't tried. Don't let them drag you down. Don't let them minimize your accomplishments.

So, what exactly were my accomplishments? I was the director of a film on Cinemax for which I had earned the enormous sum of $750 (half of which went to Tom Kane, with whom I had split the production costs). Which meant, in reality, I still had to work as a Parking PA.

But I had planted a seed with "Jean Jean and the Evil Cat," though I wouldn't see it grow for another couple of years. However, grow it did, that tiny seed, and it has continued to grow and keep me employed ever since.

Meanwhile, my PA work also benefited me. The movie (*Spike of Bensonhurst*) shot all over Brooklyn and the Bronx. As a result, I got to see a great deal of New York City, neighborhoods to which I never would have gone had I not been working: Flatbush, Williamsburg, Bed-Stuy, Bensonhurst, and the South Bronx.

In 1987, the New York City Subway trains were just starting to be treated with a special coating that repelled spray paint, a move that ended the reign of graffiti-covered trains in the city. Luckily, however, most of the trains then were still covered in what I found to be absolutely fascinating artwork. In one South Bronx neighborhood where the film shot for two weeks, I had a great view of the elevated train tracks and would sit for hours watching the art roll by (in between telling people not to park, of course).

I never made a tag with spray paint myself, but I began imitating the style on paper with markers. I think graffiti is an important art form, and when New York installed the paint-resistant trains, the city lost an amazing, unique, energetic, ever-changing art museum.

BLOODHOUNDS

A couple of months after that movie wrapped, I got work on another low-budget film. Like *Lemon Sky*, this one was for PBS' *American Playhouse*, and it starred many big-name actors who were doing it for prestige.

Bloodhounds of Broadway had a young director named Howard Brookner who died of AIDS before it was completed. A tragic story? On one level, absolutely. But I prefer to look at it like this: The last thing Howard did in his life was write and direct a feature-length motion picture starring Madonna, Randy Quaid, Matt Dillon, Esai Morales, Julie Haggerty, Jennifer Grey, and Rutger Hauer (with a cameo by William S. Burroughs). To the end, he worked at something he loved—and at a very high level. And he died before the completion bond company utterly ruined the movie.

While I was PAing on that film, my BU compatriots and I, along with some new New York colleagues, were putting together our own feature, live-action guerrilla style. It was a mockumentary about a filmmaker whose career spanned the history of film, from the 1920s to the 1970s.

Coincidentally, *Bloodhounds of Broadway* was set in the 1920s, and we seized the opportunity to shoot period sequences of our own movie on the *Bloodhounds* set, using wardrobe from the film as well as lights, props, etc.

We'd work all day as production assistants, then stay back on the set at night and shoot. We used black-and-white Super 8 film which, with its graininess, came out looking like period footage. We shot some great scenes on those sets. Then Howard, the director, found out about it.

One of the wardrobe girls came up to me on set one day and said, "Howard found out you guys are shooting your movie on the sets."

My immediate thought was, "Hmm, I guess I need to find a new job."

But she continued. "He told me to tell you whatever wardrobe you need, just ask me, and you can use it. And after the film wraps you can take a lot of it, too."

So there it was. Howard Brookner, a guy who made it to the level where he could direct a feature, instead of being stingy with his success, was spreading it around. Helping other people out. Which brings me to another really big lesson: WHEN YOU'RE SUCCESSFUL, SPREAD IT AROUND!! You might not get rewarded for it, but it's a cool thing to do. I was never able to do anything for Howard. But I like to pay his generosity forward at every opportunity. Remember—never let that spirit die!

Our mocumentary never got completed, but we got lots of international press for it because we hired Jake LaMotta to play Robert De Niro in it. And a few years later, Jake would play a major role in one of my most successful films.

But let's not go that far ahead yet.

THE WORLD OF ANIMATION BECKONS AND I IGNORE IT

While all this illicit filming was taking place, Charles Samu called me one day to tell me that he had licensed "Jean Jean and the Evil Cat" to a West Coast distributor and the film was playing at universities in California. The distributor wanted a sequel; could I come up with one?

It was an excellent opportunity for me; I see that in retrospect. But at the time, my heart wasn't in it. I wanted to do my live-action feature and so only worked half-assed on some animation ideas, when, like Homer Simpson, I should have been using my whole ass.

The West Coast distributor was not impressed with my new ideas and so didn't ask me to make another film.

A few months later, I decided to move to Los Angeles. Right before I left New York, I got to direct a couple of live-action shorts for a Nickelodeon series called *Eureeka's Castle*. It was a great way to leave. I had been in New York for two years, and I entered and exited as a paid director for network television. Never mind the crap in between!*

So, you may be asking yourself, in the words of my former classmate, "How'd you manage *that?*"

Well, first off, it wasn't a great paying situation. I don't remember how much I made, but it was similar to the amount I got from Cinemax.

However, like the Cinemax deal, it was another case where I was a paid director on a major network, which I thought was a pretty cool thing for a recent college graduate to be.

But let's get back to *how* I got into the situation: connections. Much success in the entertainment industry comes from knowing someone. So, know lots of people and your odds for success improve.

In this case, the connection I had was one I made two years earlier, in Boston on *Lemon Sky*. The stage manager on that job, Kevin Delaney, was part of a crew of people who had come up from New York to work on the production.

---

* Get it? Like really good key drawings with bad inbetweens. See Chapter Three of the instructional part.

When the film neared completion, Kevin mentioned some short films he wanted to make, I procured cameras and editing facilities from school, and we made the films. I established myself as someone who got things done rather than someone who merely had lots of plans and dreams.

When I moved to New York, Kevin was location manager on *Spike of Bensonhurst*. Remembering me as someone who could be relied upon to get things done, he got me the parking PA job. Likewise, he was location manager on *Bloodhounds*, and that's how I got that job. He was also part of the guerrilla mockumentary team.

Not long after *Bloodhounds* wrapped, Kevin produced some shorts for *Sesame Street* directed by a man named Todd Kessler (who is now famous for creating the show *Blue's Clues*).

Todd's next venture was to create several live-action bits for *Eureeka's Castle*, and he sought people to direct some of them for small budgets. He put Kevin in charge of hiring directors and I was one of the ones he hired.

Eureeka's Castle was a job in 1989 that had its roots in a job from two years earlier. I was a lowly intern in 1987, but by 1989 I was a lowly director—all because of a connection made as an intern.

But I digress.

Shortly before I moved to Los Angeles, I received a check in the mail from Charles Samu for license fees from the California distributors (whom he did not name). A week later, I read in *Variety* that he committed suicide. I never knew why. He was a very generous and helping person, and his suicide was and is a complete mystery to me. However, I try to spread his generous spirit around whenever I can.

Lesson: YOU NEVER REALLY KNOW WHAT'S GOING TO HAPPEN NEXT, DO YOU?

CHAPTER 19

Flashback to Age Nine

Instead of going to California right now, let's go back to Boston, back when I was nine years old and a connoisseur of *Monty Python's Flying Circus.*

While I enjoyed everything about the Monty Python style of humor, I particularly enjoyed Terry Gilliam's animations. Watching them, I used to think to myself, "That's *easy!* He's just cutting up paintings and moving them around under the camera. I could do that!"

So, naturally, it wasn't long before I took a pair of scissors and headed straight for my mother's prized coffee-table book of the art of Leonardo da Vinci. My goal? To make a film of the Mona Lisa blowing her nose. I thought that would just be the greatest thing ever. Unfortunately, mom caught me before I could cut up the book.

A few months later, I took a summer-school course in filmmaking. I learned the most valuable lesson of my animation career there: THERE ARE 24 FRAMES PER EVERY SECOND OF FILM. The teacher was an independent filmmaker who later headed the film department at Emerson College. His name was Bruce Cronin. Can you imagine the luck of being taught by a professional filmmaker at the age of nine? That's why I teach elementary, middle school, and high school kids in addition to college: I know how important the *right* knowledge is to budding filmmakers. A lot of teachers who teach film to younger kids don't know what they're doing. They don't know basic things like 24 frames per second.

But Bruce Cronin did, *and* he made sure we did too.

The first assignment he gave us was one where we drew with markers directly onto clear film leader.* We had to animate frame by frame right on the film. Nothing fancy, just bouncing dots, words, etc. But it taught us to respect that every second of film is made up of 24 frames. If I wrote my name on one frame, I had better put it on at least the next five if I wanted it to register at all on the screen.**

This lesson gave me a sense of timing, and I was only nine years old with no idea I'd really be an animator one day. The concept is extremely important, which is why I made the first exercise in this book very similar to the film leader exercise. You need to see for yourself how many frames it takes for something to register on screen. This helps, for example, when you want to time a character's reaction. One frame is not enough. Is eight? Maybe, if you want it brief. Maybe you need 24 frames. That's only a second. Get used to it! I know I've said this already, but it is IMPORTANT!

From drawing on film we moved to stop-motion animation with cut-outs. So, once again I went for mom's Leonardo book. But this time she offered a suggestion: I could bring the book to school to film with, but I was *not* to cut it up. If I wanted the Mona Lisa to blow her nose, I could create a separate arm holding a tissue, place it *over* the painting and animate that.

After mulling this over, I decided it wasn't a trick and that it would work, and I got to make my masterpiece. For the first time in my life, I felt artistic satisfaction.

A few years later my family bought a VCR, and I had my very own tape on which I recorded a collection of animated shorts from *Sesame Street* and animated openings to old sitcoms like *Bewitched* and *I Dream of Jeannie*. I don't know why exactly I did this, but I have referred to that tape many times as a professional. Of course, now that

---

* In this digital age, some of you might not know what film leader is. A Film Leader is the head of a movie studio. And a Clear Film Leader is a studio head who is particularly adept at getting his ideas across.

Actually, film leader is blank film, usually used at the beginning or end of a reel of film to thread through the projector before and after the actual movie. Clear film leader is completely transparent and easy to draw on with markers.

** We followed this lesson with a similar one using black film leader. Black leader is clear leader dyed black (though it could also refer to Malcolm X). This you draw on with a pin or needle, scraping off dye. Then you can color the scraped-off areas if you wish. Norman McClaren is a famous Canadian animator who made films using this technique.

we have YouTube, there's no need, but since I worked for many years *before* YouTube, the tape served me well.

In your work, don't be afraid to refer to your influences while creating. What you produce is a filtered summation of what you like, so stay in touch with the muse!

CHAPTER 20

Los Angeles/*Hip Hop Toonz*

My first summer in New York, I made friends with another PA. I was a Run DMC fan and he had grown up a few blocks from their neighborhood. He endeavored to expand my knowledge of hip-hop. We were working in the South Bronx (which I hadn't realized was the birthplace of hip-hop) on the edge of a bombed-out, burnt-down wasteland that has since been cleared away.

Our work was nocturnal, making sure no one used the cover of night to park in the area. I remember distinctly one night while sitting on the hood of a car, watching the street, he played "I'm Bad" by LL Cool J. I hadn't heard LL at that point, but I thought it was great track.

What I *thought* I was going to do . . .

Three years later, in Los Angeles, I was creating a cartoon called *Road Kill*, about a punk-rock band made up of three obnoxious orange weasels.

Once I heard a priest say, "How do you make God laugh? Tell him what you're going to do tomorrow" (he said that in an interview the night of the World Trade Center attacks). The point is, *Road Kill* was my plan, but *Hip Hop Toonz* is what I did.

. . . and what I ended up doing.

What was *Hip Hop Toonz*? It all started at Cassandra's house. That was the hangout in Hollywood amongst my friends. My friend Dave (who played me LL in the Bronx) knew Cassandra through a friend. It seemed like everyone gravitated to her house.

She was a talent manager at the time, managing the group Club Nouveau, as well as Tracy Camilla Johns and the L.A. Posse.

Who were the L.A. Posse? They were the rap production group that made LL Cool J's *Bigger and Deffer* and *Walking with a Panther* albums. They made the track for "I'm Bad," which I had admired so much in the South Bronx three years earlier. Now I was hanging out with them.

One of the producers, Muffla, had an idea for an animated TV series. Cassandra asked me if I was interested in helping out. I said of course.

In the meantime, I had found out that the mysterious West Coast distributor who had been showing "Jean Jean and the Evil Cat" was Spike and Mike's Festival of Animation.* I had been in contact with them, gotten more money (since they had been showing the film without my permission), and been commissioned to make a sequel.

---

* For the unaware, Spike and Mike's Festival of Animation and Spike and Mike's Sick and Twisted Festival of Animation are roving collections of underground animated films that play in major cities across North America. *Beavis and Butthead* first appeared in the festival, as did *South Park*. Definitely worth checking out if you can.

When I left New York, I was still trying to make a live-action feature. But now I was focusing on animation. I had taught myself to draw by this point (originally, it hadn't even occurred to me that drawing was important in animation), spending at least an hour a day sketching and more time doing animation exercises.

I was the closest thing to a real animator that Cassandra knew, and that's why she got me and Muffla working together. His idea was a hip-hop cartoon taking place in a neighborhood recording studio, based loosely on the Chung King House of Metal where L.A. Posse had worked in New York with LL Cool J and Whodini.

The series was called *Moe Bass the Fresh MC*. Muffla's apartment was filled with platinum albums and other awards. I was like, "Wait, *you* made all these records? You made the track to 'Beats to the Rhyme' [by Run DMC]? *DAYAMN*!!"

Dudley, voiced by Ice T, with Crossfade the cat.

He asked what we needed to do to get the cartoon sold and I said, "Can you get a big-name rapper to do a voice?" He got Ice T.

Dave meanwhile had met Faizon Love, who was currently doing the voice of Robin Harris in *Bebe's Kids* (the animated feature from Paramount Pictures). So we got Faizon to do another voice, wrote and recorded a script with the main characters playing the dozens* (as a way to introduce their personalities), and then I animated it. By my damn self. On equipment I built myself. And back then I had to use cels, too (see first half of book).

Ten years ago, I could have put a very useful and practical section in this book on how to photocopy animation cels cheaply on your own. But since cels are obsolete now, I'll only touch on the subject.

---

* The dozens, as in "Your mama's so stupid she wrote her autobiography about a Cadillac."

At the time, it cost between $1.25 and $2.00 per cel to have drawings professionally Xeroxed onto them. But I got the price down to 17¢ per cel. I bought transparencies from an office supply catalog and, late at night, would go into Kinko's, tape an animation peg bar on the machine, fill the paper tray with cels, and do them like that. I used registration marks to line the cels up properly, then taped peg hole strips to them. And it worked! No need to be so clever now, of course, with digital ink and paint. And thank the Lord!*

I have painted so many cels in my time, I am so grateful for the digital technology which allows me to never have to do it again. It's tedious, exacting, and if your cat decides to jump on the table while you're working, you have to stop, wash cel paint out of the cat's fur, clean the table, try to save the damaged cels, and make note of which ones you have to Xerox again. Soon you learn to lock the cat in another room while you're working.

However, painting cels and seeing the animation again, frame by frame in that state, once more reinforces valuable timing lessons.

Luckily, on this project, I got some cel painting help. There were thousands of cels, so Muffla got some people to help and moved the operation from my apartment to his office at the world-famous corner of Hollywood and Vine. Today, that building is a very fashionable upscale location with fancy restaurants on the ground level.

Back when we were there, it had twenty five year-old carpets, drop acoustical ceilings, and elevators that felt like they were powered by a hamster in a wheel. But it was five times cheaper to rent space then, the building was more than half vacant, and the hamster had a great sense of humor and could get us floor seats for Lakers games.** And we basically had the run of the whole building.

Home base was a suite of offices on the seventh floor. L.A. Posse had one office, Revenge Records had another, Get Real Productions had a third, Cassandra had moved her offices into a fourth, and the last room was a recording studio. Using the reception area, Muffla's office, and Cassandra's office, we had space for all our cel painters and plenty of room for the cels to dry.

But this was far from a tranquil, idyllic setting. I could write a book just about that office at Hollywood and Vine.

---

* You're welcome, Walter. By the way, if you're done with my *Soprano*'s DVD, can I have it back? Thanks! "G"

** Actually, Norm Nixon, who was Muffla's manager, used to sometimes give us Clippers tickets. But he wasn't a hamster, nor did he provide power for the elevator.

Musicians and rappers were coming in and out at all times. There was a group from Oakland down there for a while, and there was this kid who hung with them (I won't use his real name) called Timmy. Timmy lived in the office next to our suite. He broke into it, took some leftover sound-proofing foam from the studio to sleep on, and had his own little spot.

Timmy would use Muffla's phone after hours (unbeknownst to anyone), and make long-distance calls. Muffla would wonder why his phone bills were so high. So he'd lock his office whenever he wasn't there. Still the bills were high. Then he noticed black streaks on the wall outside his door. This was an old-fashioned office from the 1920s. Above the door was a small window that opened. Timmy had been climbing the wall and going into the office via the window.

So Muffla started locking the handset from the phone in his desk. Timmy found it. Finally the problem was solved by putting the handset on the ledge outside the window. Timmy never looked there.

All that exposition was so you can get an idea about Timmy. Sneaky. Hyper. Loyal to himself only. Impulsive. Now picture this: We're painting cels on a rainy Sunday. It's Marathon day in Los Angeles and the race passes right by the building. Timmy discovers this and gets excited, bolts into the room in which we have the cels laid out to dry and shouts, "The Marathon is outside!" before running to the window.

He happened to have a Styrofoam container of pork fried rice in his hand, which, when he stepped on a cel and slipped, went flying through the air, landing all over dozens of completed cels.

Ah, Timmy. Thanks for the help, man!

A SIDE STORY

This little tale here is very sensational and tangentially related to animation, so I feel justified in including it.

One day there was a female rapper in the studio. We'll call her Lucy, though her real name was Mary, though it was really neither. She was very pushy. I walked into the office and she introduced herself to me by announcing that she was going to be in our cartoon. I said okay, I'm sure we could find a part for her. "Uh uh" she said, shaking her head. "I want my own character. And it's got to be *important*."

Now, I'm sure none of you have heard of Lucy. Or Mary. Or her real name. Because in terms of fame, she is nobody. Meaning that back then, when she demanded all this, she was nobody as well. But I think you get a sense of her personality (pushy, rude, selfish), and you will be able to see how she caused the subsequent trouble she did.

A friend of Cassandra's was living in another city at this point. We'll call her Marita. Marita and Lucy hated each other. And on this day Marita called the office and Lucy answered. Lucy was rude to Marita and when Marita talked to Cassandra she asked why the hell that bitch was at the office.

Marita used to date a very important hip-hop mogul whose name is Victor (as much as Marita was named Marita). And so did Lucy. And they were both very fierce in their devotion to their ex boyfriend.

So much so that Marita hung up and called Victor and yelled at him: "Why is your bitch Lucy hanging out at my friend's office?"

Victor, thinking, "Do I need this drama?" called Cassandra and yelled at her to control her damn friends. He didn't need Marita calling him up and bothering him like that. He was too important for that.

Cassandra, who was trying to get her work done, told Victor, "I have nothing to do with this. Besides, you ain't all that."

Victor's response was a very cerebral one. "I ain't all that, huh? I ain't all that? We'll just see who's all that!" And he hung up.

Now, I must confess that what follows is all secondhand info because while it was happening I went to pick up Cassandra's son from school. When I came back, everyone in the office was quiet, mumbling, "I can't believe that just happened."

I kept asking "Well, what happened?" and they kept saying, "Naw, you don't wanna know."

But I *did* want to know. And finally someone told me: Victor and a very, very famous producer named Tonto came up to the office with automatic weapons to prove that Victor indeed was very much "all that," and perhaps a bag of chips as well.

While Victor was proving this, Muffla walked in and tried to calm things down. Eventually he got the situation under control.

All the bad feelings were forgotten and Victor and Tonto were about to leave when suddenly the door flew open and in walked Jones (not his real name), a DJ who worked with one of L.A. Posse's artists. "What up, cuz?" he exclaimed to everyone, not knowing what was happening.

Some background: "What up, cuz?" is a Crip greeting. Victor and Tonto were Bloods. So, of course, Victor pulled out his gun again and reasoned, "What up cuz? What up CUZ?!! What you mean 'What up *CUZ*?'!!"

Luckily, this new situation caused by Jones' little breach of etiquette was soon defused again by Muffla. The guns were put away and Victor and Tonto left shortly thereafter. In the movie version of this, I'm going to write it so that when Victor and Tonto come out the elevator in the lobby, I'm about to walk in with Cassandra's son. Victor will drop his hat but not notice. I'll pick it up and say, "Excuse me, sir, you dropped your hat," and hand it to him. He'll grunt his thanks and leave. Then I'll go up to the office and find out what happened, and, struck dumb, point to the elevator, then to myself, then say, "But . . ."

ALMOST ON MTV

Across the street, DJ Pooh had his offices. He was producing Ice Cube's *Predator* album at the time. He also had a similar cartoon idea to ours, and he had Ice Cube and Yo Yo in it. Rather than compete with him, we ended up combining our cartoon with his, calling the resulting project *Hip Hop Toonz.*

We wrote a second episode, this one featuring Ice Cube's character, and recorded the sound, though we never ended up filming it. I was supposed to direct Ice Cube's voice-over session, but his schedule and mine didn't coincide, so I recorded his part on the tape to show where his lines went and he came in and dubbed over it on another day. It came out very funny. I wish we had finished that.

But it looked like we didn't need to. In a newspaper interview, Pooh mentioned the series and was contacted by MTV, who were interested in producing it. *Extremely* interested. So interested that there was an issue of *TV Guide* that announced that MTV was going to do the series. I still have that issue. So close!!

But there was a dispute between Ice Cube and MTV over merchandising rights, and Ice Cube decided to forego the series. He and Pooh were about ready to make the movie *Friday* at that time, and they both had lots of money, so fuck MTV. I agreed, fuck MTV, only I needed the money.

During all the negotiations I got to know John Andrews, who was a producer at MTV. He produced *Beavis and Butthead* (the show and the movie), as well as *Daria* and some other stuff. He was kind enough to say that even though the series wasn't going to happen, his door was always open. Lots of people in the business say that to soften the blow of rejection, but John really meant it. You see, one of the hinges on his door was bent and so he couldn't close the door all the way, so, despite his best efforts, it was always open.

Regardless of that rotten joke, I thought that the whole *Hip Hop Toonz* episode was over. But a few years later, knowing John Andrews would help my career in a big way. We learned this lesson a few chapters back, but I didn't emphasize it: YOU NEVER KNOW HOW LONG IT WILL TAKE FOR A SEED TO GROW, SO DON'T DESPAIR!!

Hip Hop Toonz didn't happen, but it was a good experience for me. I jumped into a situation that logic said I should stay away from. I hadn't been to animation school, so what business did I have making a cartoon with Ice T and Ice Cube? But I *believed*, and it paid off. At the very least I could put on my resume that I had directed an animation pilot starring famous people.

STUPID IDEAS ABOUT MUTANT ALIENS

One day during production I was in an art store buying cel paint.* This guy came up to me and started asking me, "Oh, you do some animation?"

I said yes.

"Just as a hobby, of course, just fooling around, right?" He seemed very badly to want this to be the case.

"No," I said. "I'm making a cartoon right now starring Ice T and Ice Cube."

He looked at me like I was an asshole and walked away without another word. There are always going to be people out there trying to drag you down, people who want you to be a failure so then it's okay if they don't succeed. IGNORE THEM!!

Of course, when you're an animator, you will run into the exact opposite situation, and it can be equally frustrating. You'll meet people who have no problem believing you're a successful animator, and then they will tell you about their idea for an animated TV show and then try to convince you that your only purpose in life is to make their cartoon; that meeting them is what you have been waiting your whole life for and now everything is going to be okay because now you can animate their stupid idea about mutant aliens.

---

* Cel paint is a special kind of vinyl paint used to paint animation cels.

CHAPTER 21

Winter Blossoms Into Spring Into Summer

THE EVIL CAT DOES WASHINGTON

After things settled down with *Hip Hop Toonz*, I got a contract with the Spike and Mike Sick and Twisted Festival to do another cartoon with my Jean Jean and the Evil Cat characters. I had done a sequel called "The Cat, the Cow and Beautiful Fish" a couple of years earlier, and it was popular enough to warrant a third installment.

Since the original "Jean Jean and the Evil Cat" contained many elements which first appeared to me in a dream, I decided any sequel must also contain at least one surreal, crazy element from a dream.

The Orange Juice Cow.

In "The Cat, the Cow and the Beautiful Fish" I included a character called the Orange Juice Cow because one night I had a dream that I was sitting in a movie theater, watching a movie, when I was attacked by a flying Orange Juice Cow. I don't know why exactly he was an "orange juice" cow, but that's what the narrator of my dream called him.

For "The Evil Cat Does Washington," I made use of a dream I had involving then-president Bill Clinton and the Evil Cat. In the dream, Hillary found out that Bill had used the Evil Cat's litter

Hillary Clinton on her white horse.

The Abraham Lincoln Cow.

The Ronald Reagan Memorial Farting Sea Monkey.

box, and the Evil Cat used that as proof that he, and not Bill, was the true President of the United States.

As fascinating as my stupid dreams might be, however, the reason I mention this film is because of one of the ways I cheated to make it. There is a scene where the Evil Cat and the Clintons' cat Socks have sex, and I wanted them to copulate like a violent whirlwind, similar to the way the Tasmanian Devil moves.

At the time, I had no idea how to do this. And this was before I could get Looney Tunes on DVD or on the Internet. What I did was tape a Tasmanian Devil short off the TV one Saturday morning, then bring the tape to my sister's house to analyze it. She had a VCR that allowed frame-by-frame viewing (a feature which is pretty standard with DVD players today but was uncommon in 1994), and I needed it to carefully break down the action.

After finding a sequence where the Tasmanian Devil does his whirlwind bit, I paused on the first frame, sketched it on a piece of paper, then repeated the process for about fifteen more frames. After that, I transposed what I learned to my characters and finished the scene.

Today, there are easier and more accurate ways to similarly rip off animation, and a little later, I will actually talk about them.

THE HAPPY MOOSE

After "The Evil Cat Does Washington," I made "The Happy Moose," which is my most successful short film in terms of both critical acclaim and popularity. Many people track me down every year wanting a copy of it.

That film had a long, painful birth. Its genesis was simple enough: the main character would be a bull called the Raging Bull, and he would be voiced by Jake LaMotta.

By the way, it always surprises me that some people don't know this, but in 1980 Martin Scorsese made an amazing movie called *Raging Bull*, based on the life of former middleweight boxing champion Jake LaMotta. So, if you didn't get it immediately, do you now see the clever bit of casting in that film, having the real Jake LaMotta do the voice of a character called the Raging Bull?

Just like a few years before when I got Jake to play Robert De Niro in my mockumentary. Of course, Robert De Niro had anticipated this and returned the favor a few years in advance by playing LaMotta in *Raging Bull*, but there's nothing wrong with recycling jokes!

Usually I got some money up front from Spike and Mike to make my movies, and in return they would own some or all of the rights. This time, however, I thought I could sell the film to HBO or Showtime, as it would be a natural to play before the Scorsese film, so I financed it myself. Which meant I kept running out of money while making it.

The first step was calling Jake in New York and asking if he'd do the film. I called him and he said he would do it but his son, Jake Jr., handled all his business. I called Jake Jr., who said it seemed like an okay deal, though he was concerned about the language and content of the film. He didn't want it to damage his father's reputation.

I toned down the language a little and told him it would probably only play in the Spike and Mike Festivals but that I might be able to sell it other places, like HBO. He said let's see.

New York in the winter is one of my favorite places to be, and that's where I was to record Jake's voice-over. My budget (which didn't exist) was not enough for us to work at a proper voice-over studio, but I found a nice, well-equipped rock and roll studio that I could afford. Jake came in and did a great job with his lines. The sound engineer was laughing her ass off. (It was later reattached, with very little scarring). She didn't even know who Jake was; she'd never heard of the movie *Raging Bull*. She just thought he was funny.

It was a successful recording. My friend Cassandra was now living in New York, so I went back to her place, slept on the floor, caught a bad cold, then got on a plane back to L.A. the next day.

Over the next six to eight months, I worked intermittently on the animation between paying jobs. Finally I finished it and sent a tape copy to Jake Jr. for approval.

THE UNHAPPY BULL

Well, he hated it. He couldn't believe how foul the language was. He maintained that his father *never* swore. It wasn't true, but I didn't want to argue the point. After a couple of days of going back and forth on the phone he finally agreed to let Spike and Mike—and *only* Spike and Mike—show it. No HBO, no Showtime. And he only agreed to Spike and Mike because his niece, who was in college, told him the Spike and Mike Festivals were harmless fun and that people expected such language and it wouldn't hurt Uncle Jake's reputation.

It was disappointing not to be able to try and get "Happy Moose" on HBO, but the film did very well in the Spike and Mike Festival and received numerous critical raves in newspapers across the country.

Shortly thereafter, however, despite the film being a critical success and fan favorite at the festivals, animation work dried up completely for me. The winter I so loved in New York had descended upon my career.

DELIVERY BOY

For a year I worked as a messenger. Since I was in Los Angeles, where most of the business is entertainment-related, almost all of my deliveries were to entertainment companies. Many times, I went to offices that I used to do business with as a director. Now I was going in through the service entrance.

One day during this messenger phase, I had a meeting at HBO (I was still *trying*, you see). I took a two-hour lunch for it. A week later I was back at the same office, this time as a messenger, going to the mailroom via the service elevator. Weird, huh?

Artistically, however, I was still happy. I was playing in a hip-hop band (called 4 or 5 Dopes) at the time, so I had a creative outlet. And the combination of band and messenger job led to a funny little adventure.

CLIVE BABY

One day I was told to go to an editing suite to pick up a copy of a rough cut for Whitney Houston's latest music video. My instructions were to bring it to the Beverly Hills Hotel and make sure the front desk gave it *directly* to Clive Davis (then-head of Arista Records).

Well, I knew that this was too good an opportunity to pass up. I always had a few copies of my band's CD with me, so I decided to slip one in with the Whitney video.

Excited, I pulled my car over to the side of the road. I had to think, quickly, of the best way to do this. First, I needed a bigger envelope than the one Whitney's video was in. But where to get one?

I looked out of my car to see where I was, and I just happened to have parked in front of a shipping supply store. Awesome! I bought an envelope, wrote a note to "Clive Baby" from "D.G." (for "David Geffen," and why not?), telling him to check out this great new group. Then I put the package together with my CD and brought it to the hotel. I told the concierge that the package was one Mr. Davis was anxiously awaiting and that it must get to him personally, immediately. The concierge had been expecting it and rushed it off to Clive.

We never got signed to Arista, but I know Clive passed the CD on to one of his vice presidents because a few months later, when our manager sent some new material to Arista, the gentleman said, "Oh yes, I remember liking their album." The only way he would have had our album is if Clive Baby had given it to him.

I told one of my fellow messengers (who was also a musician) about this. He said, "Dude, you shouldn't have done that. You could have been *fired*!" Amazing the lack of vision some people have. Who cares about being fired from some crap-ass job? I had a chance to put my CD right into Clive Davis' hands and I did it. 4 or 5 Dopes didn't get signed, but I *tried*!

While that story didn't involve animation, it did illustrate the guerrilla mentality of seizing opportunities whenever and however they arise. You must sometimes make split-second decisions (risky ones), because certain opportunities only happen once in a lifetime. For example, I've never had cause to deliver anything directly to Clive Davis again.

SIGNS OF SPRING

After about a year as a messenger, I was on the Warner Bros. Hollywood lot, waiting for someone to show up and sign for a package. I had to wait for about an hour in an empty office, which was nice, because I got to take a break and get paid for waiting.

I thumbed through one of the issues of *Daily Variety* that was lying around and found a review of my friend Sloan Robinson's performance in a play about Dorothy Dandridge.

Despite being happy to see that she got a glowing review, I realized I missed being in the game. I was becoming tired of cranky entertainment executives calling me stupid for being five minutes late with a package.

As I reflected on this, my pager went off. It was a call from Jan Cox, who had been a producer at Spike and Mike. She was putting together a new animation festival for Manga Entertainment/Palm Pictures and wanted me to create a film for it.

I recognized this as a very important opportunity and immediately set about writing and storyboarding a new film. I focused all my energy into the idea, then submitted the boards to Manga, along with a budget that would allow me to leave my lucrative messenger job.

They accepted the budget and loved the concept, and suddenly I was back in action. Manga also wanted to buy "The Happy Moose" and had me dub in a new voice for the bull so as not to run afoul of the LaMottas.

I was so happy to be earning money as an animator again that for $3,000 I joyously sold Manga the entire rights, for all eternity, to "The Happy Moose." What a chump I was! But I was happy at the moment.

Lesson: DON'T SELL ANYTHING AWAY FOREVER FOR LESS THAN ONE MILLION DOLLARS!!!

Luckily, Manga later failed to provide royalty statements such as was stipulated in our contract, so that breach meant I got my rights back. But things don't usually work out that way.

While recording the soundtrack for the new film, called "Attack of the Hungry Hungry Nipples," I decided to utilize 4 or 5 Dopes so as to get some synergetic cross-promotion going on. At the time our DJ was DJ Kilmore (who is now in Incubus), and the music came out very nice, with some excellent turntable work on it. In fact, I still get several e-mails a year from people wanting a copy of the title song.

The Hungry Hungry Nipples with the Flying Richard Nixon Baseball Bat.

That was the last film I worked on where I had no postproduction budget. I always recorded the sound for my films before animating, hoping the timing would make for good animation, but I never had the budget to make edits afterwards. Hence, I feel all my films up to and including that one could use some editing to tighten them up. But back then I was working on 35 mm film, which was too expensive for me to cut (or reshoot).

In this glorious new digital age, postproduction is easy and cheap and I hope you all are grateful!!!

SEEDS PLANTED IN THE PAST BEGIN TO GROW

A month before the film's release, the World Animation Celebration was held in Pasadena. On the closing night, animation studios were invited to have their in-house bands play in a battle of the bands. So 4 or 5 Dopes played, representing Evil Cat Studios (my company), and one of the judges was John Andrews, formerly of MTV, now running the commercial division of Klasky Csupo. We talked briefly after the show—nice to see you again, too bad the hip-hop cartoon didn't work out with MTV, but how've you been?—and all that kind of stuff. With John, however, it was never phony. Or if it was, dude totally fooled me.

About a week later, John called me to see if I wanted a job as a layout artist at Klasky Csupo. I declined, though I made sure he knew I appreciated the offer. But I only wanted to be a director. I guess I was playing hardball, but it's easy to take a hard line if you'd rather work at Wal-Mart than be a layout slave.

A few weeks later, *General Chaos* (the Manga Festival) opened in theaters. John Andrews attended one of the screenings. He was impressed both with my film and with the audience response it got, and he called me again. Would I like to sign with Klasky Csupo as a director? Yes. Yes, I could do that.

CHAPTER 22

A Vegetarian at McDonald's

MCDONALD'S

Immediately John had me up for a job, an anti-smoking PSA. I prepared some sample art and animation but, alas, was not awarded the job. But I put a lot of work into the bid, and that proved I was serious.

A couple of weeks later, John asked me to come up with character designs and storyboards for a series of McDonald's ads. I was excited by the concept: a secret agent named Agent M (when I was little I'd had a stuffed monkey named Agent M) who worked with a sarcastic cat named Sidecat as a sidekick. It was perfect for me. I love spy movies, and most of my films to date had starred a sarcastic cat.

I also happen to be a vegetarian, but I didn't consider that to be a conflict at the time. When I was a kid, McDonald's was my favorite restaurant in the world, so everything seemed warm and fuzzy and perfect.

I did many designs and storyboards, and packaged it all in a dossier stamped with the McDonald's logo, underneath which was written "McBureau of Intelligence." It looked *tight*, and I got it done well before the deadline.

Then, before I had a chance to submit anything, John called and said, "It doesn't look like the McDonald's project is going to happen. The corporate people don't want to go with the concept."

"But," I protested, "I did all this work! It looks *tight*!"

"Well, if it looks *tight*," said John, "let's send it to the agency anyway."

Good thing we did, because the agency loved the designs, and their passion for the project was renewed and they decided to re-approach corporate. They made giant stand-ups of the characters and brought them to the meeting and sold the idea. We got five spots out of it and I started making really good money for the first time in my life.

Lesson: YOU CAN BRING THINGS BACK TO LIFE, OR TRY ANYWAY, EVEN WHEN THE ANSWER IS SUPPOSED TO BE NO.

It was a fun project, for the most part. I suggested that we hire Adam West (the original Batman) to do Agent M's voice. They hired him. I suggested Taurean Blacque, who played detective Neil Washington on *Hill Street Blues*, to voice the cat. Taurean was hired. People were taking my suggestions seriously. It felt good. The agency hired actress Khandi Alexander (who was then the star of *News Radio* and later went on to do an amazing performance in HBO's *The Corner*) to do the voice-over announcing. Quite a formidable cast!

These particular spots played mainly in the South, where the McDonald's restaurants supplemented them with cups, posters, and other promotional items featuring my characters.

This is when I learned that I have a distinctive drawing style. A friend of mine came back from Atlanta and told me, "Dude, you need to get a lawyer. McDonald's totally ripped off your Evil Cat character!" He didn't know I had done the spots, but he saw my drawings on a billboard and recognized them as something I would have done. Sidecat didn't really look like the Evil Cat, but he could tell I drew it.

DIFFERENT PERCEPTIONS AT KLASKY CSUPO

Having entered a major studio as a director and not as someone who worked his way up from the bottom, I encountered resistance and hostility at Klasky Csupo. Especially since I had a guerrilla attitude towards things.

Therefore, some of the animators I was directing didn't do things I asked them to do. Like when I gave them a mouth chart for the characters. Since the characters were of my unique style, their mouths had special shapes for dialogue. One animator—let's call him Biff—refused to follow the mouth chart. He had drawn all his A mouths in a generic Animation 101 style. I asked him to refer to the chart and change all the A mouths.

Stylized mouth vs. traditional mouth.

Biff refused. Referring to my As, he said, "That's not how you draw an A."

I told him, "For this character, that *is* how you draw an A, so just change them, it won't take long." He muttered something as he went away. A few days later, I got the scene back from cleanup and looked at it, and saw that the As hadn't been changed. So I had to erase and fix them all myself. I could have made a big deal about it, but I didn't.

Another director at Klasky was very resentful of my presence. She didn't like that I lacked formal drawing training. She would tell the other animators that I was a terrible artist, and they in turn became less inclined to listen to what I said.

I think insecurity is why people try to drag you down. Because there was another director at Klasky, we'll call him Tom Decker (because that's his name). Tom is extremely talented and I think he is aware of it. He never disrespected me, and comparing his artwork to mine would be like comparing Michael Jordan's basketball skills to those of a water buffalo. A very *funny* water buffalo, I'd like to think, but still with a weak jump shot and no inside game whatsoever.

I learned a great deal from Tom, and here's a lesson from him: IF YOU ARE TALENTED, BE HUMBLE AND GRACIOUS ABOUT IT.

Tom worked with Chuck Jones on several productions, which means he learned from the man I consider to be the greatest animation director ever. I animated some scenes on a production Tom was directing, and from the corrections he made to my work, I filled in many gaps in my erratic animation training.

From him I learned the finer points of overlapping action, settling, and other timing issues. It was like the masters class I never took at the animation school I never attended.

A few years prior, I had volunteered to write for and art direct the ASIFA Hollywood* magazine *The Inbetweener*. In that capacity I was able to interview two animation legends whom I greatly admire: Bill Melendez** and June Foray.*** Both were very encouraging towards my aspirations. Most ASIFA members hated my guts because I was an outsider and an upstart who wanted to make cartoons without following the rules. They made snide comments at me whenever I said I was starting my own animation company. I was doomed to failure, they said.

I meekly mentioned this to June Foray when I interviewed her. She had asked me what my connection to the business was and I said I wanted to have my own company but that everyone was telling me not to even try.

She got very indignant and told me to not listen to negative people, to believe in myself and just DO IT. Thank you, Rocky the Flying Squirrel! And I pass your wisdom on whenever I can (and praise your great talent as well)!

Bill Melendez had similar advice. I was able to visit the original studios that all the Snoopy shows were made in and meet some of the great artists who worked on the classics (such as Dean Spille, who did the amazing watercolor skies in the Charlie Brown specials, which are a big influence on my style).

GUERRILLA TACTICS ON A CORPORATE PROJECT

For the postproduction of two of the McDonald's spots, I traveled to Dallas where the ad agency was located. At the same time we were doing final editing, the agency was preparing a presentation to the McDonald's corporation to expand the ad campaign.

As part of this presentation, they had Adam West, in character as Agent M, record a message which pointed out to the McDonald's executives the URGENCY of expanding the campaign.

An hour before the presentation, we were working on the sound when one of the agency guys said it was too bad we couldn't have animated Agent M's corporate plea.

The guerrilla animator in me perked up. There was only an hour, what could we do? I immediately came up with a plan. From one of the

---

* ASIFA Hollywood is the Los Angeles branch of the International Animated Film Society.

** Bill Melendez animated for Disney and Warner Bros. in the golden era, then started his own studio which has done every single bit of Charlie Brown and Snoopy animation ever.

*** June Foray is one of the absolute greatest voice-over artists ever, voicing Warner Bros. characters and Rocket J. Squirrel, and narrating "Boobie Girl."

actual commercials, we would capture an image of Agent M's supercomputer. We would blow this up to fill the entire frame. The Flame* operator could then draw a series of squiggly lines to superimpose on Agent M's computer screen, which we would randomly change every four to six frames during Agent M's dialogue. When he was silent, we'd have a flat line. This would give the impression that Agent M's voice was being digitally transmitted through his computer.

It would not be great animation, but it would be a striking video that looked cool and, most importantly, it was doable in an hour.

The only problem was that the Flame operator was afraid to try it. But, instead of admitting his fear or that he couldn't understand the concept, he began to fuss about how it would be impossible. He wasn't an artist; how could he make squiggly lines? I showed him how. He did it.

But, he insisted, he couldn't be bothered to put the flat lines in during the silence. I said, "It will make the illusion better if you do." He insisted it would not be possible.

Then a miracle occurred. As he began to put it all together, he saw how cool it was looking. He got excited. And he saw that the flat lines would indeed help the illusion. He went and put them in during every pause.

And the whole thing came out looking fantastic—so good that I put it on my demo reel. We finished in plenty of time, the presentation went well, and everyone was happy.

That was an instance of guerrilla attitude and techniques working in the corporate world. The attitude of YES WE CAN MAKE SOMETHING HAPPEN triumphed over "There's not enough time or money." The mentality of finding a way to make something out of nothing prevailed over "I never did this before so it won't work." We cheated at the last minute, but it looked like we had planned the whole operation weeks in advance.

It was cool.

One last mention about this first venture inside the PROPER world of animation: Not only did I make way more money, I also worked way less. Ten hours a day was all that was expected of me, which was much nicer than the eighteen-plus-hour days I did on my own jobs. And I had helpers, even if they didn't always cooperate.

When you are in the mainstream, you will find people work less hard than they do in the guerrilla world. The downside of course is that you're making hamburger commercials and not what you want. But a balance is always there to be found.

---

* A Flame system is an edit bay with many sophisticated graphics capabilities.

CHAPTER 23

Sixty-Five Hours Straight

Now, right after saying that I worked way less while at Klasky Csupo, allow me to completely contradict myself.

Sometimes you have to do very difficult things and don't see the reward right away. Such was the case with a spot I directed for an online entertainment site called Den.Net. It was a theatrical spot created to play before screenings of Kevin Smith's *Dogma*.

Immediately in this case there *was* a nice reward: $9,000 for a week's work. But in order to get the spot done I had to work straight through for sixty-five hours. It's not fun to do that. Maybe the first forty-eight are okay, but. . . .

I had no idea I was going to work that long without a break. I kept thinking I'd be done in a couple of hours.

Chiat/Day, the agency who handled the Den spot, offered it to several companies. It was a minute of animation and needed to be done in one week. Completely done and output. Every studio turned them down except Klasky because I was crazy enough to take it.

That job hurt like hell to finish, but it helped me out later on, because people knew me as the guy who could get a minute done in a week. It's kind of like being known in your neighborhood as the kid who will eat bugs on a dare.

CHAPTER 24

The Stone Stanley Era

My Stone Stanley era happened at exactly the same time as the Klasky Csupo era. You see, since I only had to work ten hours a day at Klasky Csupo, I had some extra time on my hands. So I had two eras at once, and, as a result, I rarely slept. Some people burn their candle at both ends; I cut my candle open and burned it in the middle as well. It hurt my health but not my bank account. In retrospect, I must say it's okay to push oneself, but be aware that you WILL BURN OUT and will need time off. No matter how invincible you feel, overworking will knock your ass down at some point. Be ready for it!

Stone Stanley Entertainment, in case you didn't know, brought the world such TV shows as *Shop 'til You Drop*, *Love Lines*, *The Man Show*, and *The Mole*. They also tried to bring *The Instigators* to the world. Just what was *The Instigators*? *The Instigators* was a TV series starring my character the Evil Cat, who instead of solving problems of international intrigue, went out and *started* them.

Okay, so it didn't make it onto television, but there's a lesson in here. Follow the path.

I make "Attack of the Hungry Hungry Nipples" in 1997. It is released in 1998. In 1999 I get a new agent because the movie is receiving critical and popular acclaim in film festivals. This agent brings the film (along with "The Happy Moose") to Messrs Stone and Stanley. They show it around their production offices and people start repeating the cry of the Hungry Nipples ("You suck something!"). Stone and Stanley see that this is good clean infectious fun and get that it could catch on with the world at large.

So they give me a healthy sum of money and option the project from me. That means they have the rights for a year to try and sell it to a network.

We develop the series. I write seven episodes. They promote it. The Evil Cat for a brief period has the same publicity firm as Roseanne and Leonardo DiCaprio. He is way more famous than me.

Variety does a story on the series. They run a picture of the Evil Cat blowing up a building. He is WAY more famous than me.

We animate a trailer. We bring it to Comedy Central and MTV. They say no.

End of story.

What's the moral? Well, it's not that I started to hate MTV and Comedy Central, because that's not true. I had *always* hated MTV and Comedy Central.

There actually is no moral. I just wanted to give an example of one thing that can happen with a series idea. By the way, all my series have ended up like this: *close*, but never quite on television. I have two more stories like that, which I'll relate a little later. And they involve Batman again, so stay tuned.

Stone Stanley also optioned the characters from my Happy Moose short with the idea of turning it into a TV series. I made a pilot for the show, which, like *The Instigators*, did not make it onto television, but it did go on tour with the band Korn, screening in the arenas before they came onstage each night. It's a strange feeling to have your characters go on a major arena tour while you sit at home, not on tour. Kind of like when your character gets his picture in *Variety* and you don't.

One thing I must add here is that Stone Stanley was a great company. Scott Stone and David Stanley are two rare individuals in Hollywood—they have heart and soul. Their company was a fun place to be. Rock on, guys!

CHAPTER 25

Cedric the Entertainer

Although this chapter features a well-known celebrity, it's relatively short. The lesson is a good one, though.

Well-known (and very funny) comedian Cedric the Entertainer wanted to create an animated television series in 1999. Through his management team, he came to Klasky Csupo with it.

John Andrews suggested me as the director. I met the Cedric team and, while nothing bad happened during the meeting, I could tell they hated my guts by the end of it. I never found out why they hated me, but they definitely did and told John they didn't want me to direct the project.

But that's not where this chapter's lesson comes from (although "mysterious hate sometimes happens" might be a good side lesson). The lesson comes from how the project devolved from a very promising one into something too convoluted to be of any value.

Here's what happened. Originally Cedric wanted to animate a song from his comedy routine. That would have been a funny film. But then he and his team wanted to expand it to incorporate characters from his series idea so that the video would serve as a pitch film for the show.

That's when the trouble began. As soon as you start trying to make one project serve multiple needs, you put the project in peril.

It got worse. They decided to do a short episode of the series instead, which was a good idea. But that solid, focused concept soon became muddled by their attempts to make it a film that would also explain the series.

One character, a talking dog, narrated the film. He introduced all the characters. But cramming in introductions to many characters took away from any chance to tell a funny and engaging story.

By that point I was allowed to direct a small segment of the film, so I thought I would voice my opinion that the project was losing its focus. I suggested a way to introduce characters through the story rather than exposition, which I believed would make the film easier to watch.

I was ignored. The film was finished and it screened during intermissions on the Kings of Comedy Tour, an arena tour of comedians featuring Cedric. At the show I attended in Los Angeles, people were baffled by the piece as they wandered around buying beer, popcorn, and souvenirs.

I *told* them.

The lesson here is important: Don't try to make a project serve too many needs if that means it loses its focus. Something simpler and funny would have been better, even if it didn't introduce all the characters. Cedric is funny as hell, but this film wasn't. I hope he redoes it some day, makes it funny like he can, and sells it. Because an animated Cedric the Entertainer series would be great.

CHAPTER 26

The Nirvana of Noggin

One of my last jobs at Klasky Csupo was a thirty-second television and theatrical spot for Noggin. Noggin is a kids network co-created by Sesame Workshop and Nickelodeon.

Before the job, I knew nothing of Noggin. Shortly after being approached for the job, I researched the network and was surprised and impressed by its mission.

Why? Because it stressed IMAGINATION and THINKING, and while I was branded an "edgy" and "sick and twisted" animator, my personal sensibilities are actually more akin to the Muppets than *American Pie*. In fact, I was yearning to break into something more Muppet-like, and, since Noggin was half-owned by Sesame Street, I figured this was at least half a chance. (It was also half owned by MTV, which, later on, would prove to be its doom.)

At the time there was a trend in children's television to have kid hosts who were so cool they were snotty. They were like miniature mixtures of game-show hosts and car salesmen: really sleazy, conceited, and way too cool for their own good.

Watching the original programming Noggin had, I was touched by the honesty, sensitivity, and thoughtfulness of the kids on the network. There was a show where kids of different backgrounds changed places (*A Walk in Your Shoes*) and learned about each other's lives. City and country. Christian and Jew. And the comments the kids made about their experiences were smart, insightful, and a welcome change from the tiny car salesmen creeps infecting children's TV at the time.

Design-wise, the Noggin executives wanted their network to look unlike any other network. Again, I thought, "Right on!"

In the end, it was probably the most enjoyable commercial I've ever worked on. But while it was a major commercial for a major company by a major ad agency, budget-wise it was small and I had to use guerrilla techniques and attitude to get it done.

It was on this project that Seth Strong joined Klasky Csupo. He would later be part of my company Evil Cat Land. Seth knew 2D and 3D animation. The Noggin project required some 3D, but Klasky's 3D department was in its infancy then, by which I mean that nobody knew what they were doing, and the producers said we couldn't do any 3D because it was too expensive.

But Seth said, "No, it's not," and overnight he did the animation we needed. He also helped put the project together in After Effects (a new program then that I had not yet learned), enabling us to do things in the spot that were supposedly beyond our means.

That's the guerrilla way.

We also needed some special effects as background elements. I had some footage stored away that I had created while fooling around with a video camera in college. It was not generated with any high-tech software, but it looked cool. So we imported it, placed it in the commercial and, in true guerrilla fashion, finished the spot. For very little money we made it look like we had a really big budget.

CHAPTER 27

Cat Rising from the Ashes

As all good things must do, my relationship with Klasky Csupo ended in 2001. Occasionally in this business you become dead in the eyes of others, and that's what happened to me at Klasky Csupo. There came a time when the powers that be decided I was no longer an asset to the company, that my career was not viable, that I was obsolete, that I no longer mattered. I was something to be scraped off the bottom of their shoe.

And, in many ways, I felt the same way about Klasky Csupo. I felt it had become too corporate and impersonal, and there was one executive in particular who I felt was made from pure, concentrated essence of evil.

In other words, it was no longer a healthy relationship.

So I left to form a new independent venture, along with three other animators—the aforementioned Seth Strong, along with the very talented Pete Doan and Layron DeJarnette.

We called ourselves "Evil Cat Land," in honor of the character that got me into the animation business. At the time, Evil Cat Land was going to be, in addition to an animation company, a virtual theme park in cyberspace. The theme park never materialized, but the animation company has had a nice ride.

THE CAT, THE BAT, AND THE OWL

Our first move, of course, was to contact Batman. One of the last projects I worked on at Klasky was a TV series (that, like *Hip Hop Toonz*, never got made) called *Stop Calling Me Night Owl*. It was created with Adam West and had loads of promise which it never kept.

Plotting our future, we decided it might be good if we brought the *Night Owl* project with us. We contacted Adam and his agent Fred Wostbrock to see if they were into us trying to get the project made somewhere else. They were. So, we had no work yet, but we had Batman on our team.

THE CAT AND THE DUCK

As we searched for a suitable space out of which to work, a Klasky colleague, director Paul Vester, suggested we contact Duck Soup Studios because they were looking for new talent to join with.

Here's where my sixty-five hours straight on the Den spot paid off: Duck Soup had passed on that same job, and they knew that I was the crazy guy who ended up making it. I think part of why they signed us was that they knew with us on board they'd never have to turn down another job—Evil Cat would do anything; they're the guys who will eat bugs on a dare.*

They also knew we were down with Batman.

Duck Soup was very open to bringing us in as a sort of "sub studio," and we were signed as a directing team.

COOKIES AND COUCH STUFFING

Shortly thereafter, they booked us to do three spots for a Mexican snack cake called Gansito. For these we were to have an animated duck interact with live-action kids. Well, if Spielberg, Richard Williams, Robert Zemeckis, Disney, and Warner Bros. could team up to do that for *Who Framed Roger Rabbit?*, then certainly the four of us could do it.

We went to Mexico City to supervise the live-action shoots, where I ate many, many Gansitos. What were they like, you might wonder? Imagine couch stuffing with strawberry jelly and Cool Whip smeared on it, covered in stale chocolate. *Mmmmm!* I couldn't stop myself.

---

* For the record, I have never eaten bugs, on a dare or otherwise, unless you count the time when a mosquito flew in my mouth. Little bastard.

We then returned to Los Angeles and did our thing. It was a pretty mainstream production and the only guerrilla elements were that we would very often stay up for thirty hours straight and that it was on this job that I came up with the tones and highlights cheat described in the instructional section of this book.

It was demanded by the ad agency that the duck have tones and highlights. But their budget was so small and their deadline so tight, it was going to be difficult to do it the proper way.

Luckily, while experimenting on the computer a couple of weeks before, I had accidentally discovered the cheat, and so we had no trouble.

Interestingly, none of my directing peers have ever wanted to have anything to do with this cheat. I'd show them how to do it, how it really worked, and they'd all say, "It won't work." And I'd say, "I just showed you that it works." But, as they say, you can't teach an old fish how to play the cello. But *you* can learn!

Concurrently, Duck Soup was making some spots for Keebler cookies, so there were boxes upon boxes of Chips Deluxe cookies in the studio. That's pretty much all I ate some weeks—Chips Deluxe cookies. They tasted great, but I didn't feel all too healthy most days.

It makes you wonder: why do the things that we'd love to have happen when we're eight years old happen when we're thirty, when it no longer matters? I mean, when you're eight, who wouldn't want to eat cookies for all three meals? And then to have an endless supply of them? *Dayamn!** But between the Gansitos and the cookies, I'm surprised I'm alive to write this.

Overall, the job was pretty brutal. The brutality began very early. We were eager to impress, so we decided that instead of delivering storyboards on the day we were supposed to, we would deliver an animatic, which was what we were supposed to deliver the following week.

---

* Speaking of which, it's amazing how much of what would have been cool to me when I was eight happened to me by the time I was thirty but didn't have quite the same impact. When I was younger I would have loved to live in the Brady Bunch's neighborhood. I mean, who wouldn't? Then, when I moved to L.A., my apartment was a few blocks from the house they used for exterior shots in the series. But, strangely, I felt no spiritual enrichment from this.

I knew Batman. I used to see Mr. Whipple (from the old Charmin commercials) crossing the street near my home. I sat a table away from Lou Grant at a pizza restaurant. I sat a table away from Al Delvecchio at another pizza restaurant. I saw Dr. Ehrlich at the Chinese joint. I was in TV Land! And I ate cookies all the time.

But was I happy? I don't remember, actually. I was working too much!

The animatic not only showed timing for the spot, but we added color frames so everyone could get a clearer idea of the overall design and look. We also included some rough motion to show how characters would move across the screen, etc. We sent it off and sat back, content: we had made a very nice animatic and we were a week ahead of schedule. It felt nice.

The euphoria lasted a very short time. We soon got an angry phone call from the ad agency saying we what we sent them was the worst animation they had ever seen. We explained that we hadn't sent them any animation, we'd sent an *animatic*. They replied angrily that they knew what animation was and we were terrible at it. We reiterated that we hadn't sent them any animation yet.

They felt that not only were we horrible animators, we had insulted them by saying that they didn't understand the animation process.

We were unable to ever convince them that all we had sent was an animatic. As a result, they were consistently abusive to us. When we sent animation and it looked good, they said things like, "Well, that's better. Did you hire someone else to do it?"

At one point they had broken my self-confidence to the point where I wondered if I really *could* animate. So we *did* hire other animators to work on the project; really great animators whose work was beyond reproach. When the agency insulted this new work, I realized it wasn't the animation, it was the agency people. They were *evil*.

We had to travel back to Mexico City to shoot live-action footage to mix with the animation. These shoots were grueling, though they didn't have to be. For example, one day we were filming at a skate park (which was near a smoking volcano, which was cool to look at until the smog blocked it out). The park was painted by the art department after having had the style approved by the ad agency a few days earlier. But, on shoot day, with the actors in place, the cameras loaded and ready to roll, the head of the agency (we'll call her Cruella) decided she didn't like it anymore.

So the park had to be painted again. Which took *hours*. Which meant that we ran out of daylight before we could finish shooting. Which meant that many of the "daytime" shots had to be done at night, with lots of artificial light.

We had to go to Mexico City three times. By the third trip, I had less than absolutely no desire to go. When I got to the L.A. airport, I realized I had forgotten my plane ticket. I told the producer, who was also making the trip, that I guessed she had to go by herself.

She said no, I was going to have to go home and get my ticket. Which I did. I would be remiss if I didn't mention that this producer was unlike any other I have ever worked with. Almost every other producer has been an insecure, uptight, sadistic, untalented, lying bucket of squid shit. Not Sandra Oda. When I said I wasn't going to go to Mexico, she didn't panic, she didn't get tyrannical (though I was being irrational). She kept her cool as always but said I had to go.

I knew she was right. And because she was completely cool and nice the whole time, I couldn't say, "Well, fuck you, I quit." She continued to act like a reasonable, peaceful human being, and I had no choice but to follow suit.

There's another lesson here, which I think is a Gandhian principle: be the change you wish to see in others. She was setting such a genuinely high moral tone that I felt compelled to raise my own game to her level.

Still, when I returned to the airport, I wasn't exactly in a state of bliss. This was December 2001, and airport security was *tight*, which I thought was uselessly reactionary. I mean, come on, so what if I couldn't bring a plastic fork from McDonald's on the plane? I could still stab the pilot through the trachea with my number two pencil. And, being an animator, I had several of those with me.

So, as we waited in the line to be searched for plastic utensils, my mood was edgy. As we reached the front of the line, an Army soldier carrying a rifle walked past the checkpoint. I went up to the man inspecting our documents and I said, "Did you see that guy with the gun walk past you?"

The man looked alarmed. "What man with a gun?" he asked.

Pointing in the direction in which the Army guy went, I said, "That guy with the green shirt and pants. He just walked right by you and he had a rifle."

Well, the security guy was relieved when he realized I was referring to Army Guy. "Oh, that's okay," he said.

"Okay? Aren't you concerned that a man with a rifle just walked past you?"

He assured me that I had nothing to worry about and waved me through the line after checking my papers.

So here's another lesson: If you want to bring a rifle into the airport, wear an army uniform.

That incident was the closest thing to fun I had on the whole trip.

CHAPTER 28

Bruce Wayne, the Riddler, and Catwoman

This chapter probably has very little educational value, but it's included because it stars millionaire Bruce Wayne, the Riddler, and Catwoman.

I don't mean *fakes*, either. I'm not talking about actors *portraying* these characters. I'm talking about THE REAL DEAL: Adam West, Frank Gorshin, and Julie Newmar.

Not long after we returned from Mexico, we became entrenched in cranking out the Gansito animation. Oh, wow, hey, look! I found a lesson in here: how to mix hand-drawn characters with live-action actors! Cool!

Before I get to Catwoman, let me talk a little more about the Gansito Duck.

It's actually very simple to mix animated characters with live-action ones, provided you have the equipment, all of which is available for home use.

First you will need a live-action camera (film looks more professional than video, but video is easier to get your hands on). You will need a computer with a video-capture card (which allows you to digitize your live-action footage into the computer). You will need Adobe After Effects, a printer, peg hole strips, and an animation light box with a peg bar.

The only element here not covered in the first section of this book is peg hole strips, which are simply thin strips of paper punched with animation holes.

Here's what you do. Shoot a live-action scene into which you want to insert a cartoon character. Make sure your actors leave space in their acting for the animated character to be added later. At this stage they must interact with an *imaginary* character. They must *pretend* the character is there.

Having shot your footage, import it into your computer, then import it into After Effects. After Effects will let you export each frame as a JPEG, which you can then print from Photoshop. You should do so. If you use After Effects' time code function, each frame will be automatically numbered, which will help avoid the frustrating sort of chaos that even anarchists dislike.

On your light box, take the first printout, lay it down, and tape a peg strip to it. Keep this drawing (professionally known as a "roto") on the light box and use the border around it to align each subsequent drawing as you tape peg strips to them.

Once this is done you simply place blank animation paper over each roto and animate your character interacting with real life. Once you're happy with the drawings, clean them up, scan them, paint them, export them with an alpha channel, bring them into After Effects, and drop them over the live-action footage. You might want to use masks at some point if your animation goes behind any of the live-action elements.

Later in the Gansito job we also used rotos to cheat. We were requested to make the Duck's movement in one scene look like Baloo the Bear's action in a specific scene from Disney's *Jungle Book*. So we printed the scene from *Jungle Book* out frame by frame and traced our character over the action. We had to make modifications—we had a duck instead of a bear—but the timing from the Disney movie was excellent and copying it saved us lots of time. I'm not saying you should copy everything all the time, but then again, why not? It worked well for us.

Using the rotos to steal animation, by the way, was an updated version of the procedure I used to figure out Tasmanian Devil motion back on "The Evil Cat Does Washington."

So, wow. That was a nice lesson! No real need to talk about Catwoman and the Riddler now, is there?

CHAPTER 29

Bruce Wayne, The Riddler, and Catwoman (Really)

Oh, wait, you *do* want to hear about Catwoman? Okay. Just calm down, I'll tell you.

While we were in the midst of animating the Gansito Duck, we were also coordinating the *Stop Calling Me Night Owl* project. We had a short pilot animation we wanted to do, and we needed Adam West to do the voice-over. And Frank Gorshin (the Riddler), if possible. After a couple of aborted attempts at coordinating our schedule with Adam and Frank's (as well as trying to get into a recording studio at the last minute), we were able to do the voices on the set of a TV Land promo shoot.

The original *Batman* series was about to be launched on TV Land, so they had most of the original cast come down to do some funny little interstitials to promote it.

In between taping their spots, Adam and Frank recorded their voices for us. It wasn't an ideal situation—we had to do the recording in the makeup room and record it onto videotape—but the quality was good enough in the end.

Both Adam and Frank were very funny. And we saw Catwoman (Julie Newmar) a few times as well that day, prowling around between her tapings. She was nice.

Soon after we finished recording, Layron and I were talking to Frank in a corridor. And, wouldn't you know, an uptight, type-A producer burst onto the scene. "Frank, you have to do an interview right now!" she demanded.

Frank replied that he would do it in a few minutes, he was unwinding. Ms. Type-A got more upset. "It has to be now!" I think had she not been so keyed up, Frank would have gone willingly in the first place. But he said he wanted to finish his cigarette.

So I said to the woman, "It's okay. *I'll* do the interview." And I started towards where she had indicated Frank must go. "Come on."

Ms. Type-A was taken aback. She looked me up and down as if she were surveying a pile of garbage and said "And who are you?" with all the politeness of Dick Cheney.

"I'm Frank Junior," I replied with an "I thought everyone knew that" tone.

That stunned her a bit. "What?" she said. "Huh? I didn't—" Frank burst out laughing.

I let her try and get her bearings for a minute, then said, "No, I'm just kidding." Her face, which had been trying to find some sort of pleasant or apologetic kind of look, reverted to its usual evil glow as she realized she could freely treat me like garbage again since I wasn't related to anyone famous.

And that's what happened.*

---

* In general, beware of anyone who walks around with a clipboard and/or a walkie-talkie. Chances are they will yell at you.

CHAPTER 30

Doing Time in Las Vegas

After Gansito, we were invited to bid on an interesting project for MGM Hotels in Las Vegas. It was an eight-minute piece starring the heads of all the MGM Hotels as superheroes.

Klasky Csupo was the other company MGM/Mirage was considering for the project, and I felt that if we got the gig it would prove that, despite the opinions of the executives at Klasky Csupo, my career was not over, that I was not dead, obsolete, or something to be scraped from the bottom of a shoe.

We did some sample animation in a few different styles that the MGM people had suggested. We had very limited time, but knowing guerrilla tactics we were able to move swiftly and efficiently, reusing and adapting preexisting animation we had lying around until we had a very impressive presentation piece. Three days after we heard about the job, we flew to Las Vegas to pitch our idea.

Klasky Csupo did no special animation for their pitch; they merely showed some previous work one of their directors had done. And that's why we got the job. We made a much bigger effort and had more enthusiasm. We were genuinely excited when we got the job, and we made sure the MGM/Mirage executives knew it. So there's a good lesson: If you're up for a job, WANT IT, and let 'em know you want it.

CHAPTER 31

Cheating Las Vegas

The budget for the MGM project was small but comfortable. But it was only comfortable because of all the cheats we knew. For example, all the backgrounds were made from photographs run through Photoshop filters. We went all around the Las Vegas Strip and took photos from all the angles we needed for the film, then doctored them in Photoshop until we had a unique cartoon-y style that looked, well, awesome.

The MGM establishment gave us access to usually forbidden areas of the hotels so we could get shots of executive suites as well as shots from extreme overhead angles, etc.

My favorite part was when I had to lie down in the middle of Las Vegas Boulevard one night to get a striking low-angle shot of the Flamingo Hotel.

MGM/Mirage were great people to work with. They gave us great hotel rooms and tickets to Cirque de Soleil, and they paid us on time. I liked them.

CHAPTER 32

The Award-Winning "Win For Life"

When I first went to Duck Soup, I let them know that in addition to directing and animating, I also composed music. If they ever had a project where they needed top-rate music for little money, I asked them to please keep me in mind.

A little while after the MGM job, Duck was bidding on a thirty-second TV ad for the Ohio Lottery to promote its new "Win For Life" scratcher game. They had another director in mind but thought I might be able to do the music. I was excited by this prospect.

After a week or so of pitches to the ad agency, Duck Soup's executive producer Mark Medernach told me it looked like the job wouldn't happen because the budget was too small and the deadline was too tight.

I asked what the budget and deadline were and he told me it was $20,000 and two weeks. Now, to most directors that *is* too small and too tight. But to me and Evil Cat Land, it's bloody luxury! I said we could do it, no problem. Suddenly, instead of just a music job, we had the whole spot.

That is, if the agency accepted us.

The agency had come up with a very simple but funny, concise, clear, and effective story. A lot of times, what the agency gives you is half-baked or has too many elements for thirty seconds or is just BAD. But this spot was well-conceived from the start, and I told them so when we had our phone conference. I said I knew the spot would turn out well because it would be built on a very solid foundation.

That's the kind of thing you're always supposed to tell an agency when trying to get a project, but this time I was being honest. In fact, I am incapable of bullshitting a client. I just can't do it. If I think the project is stupid, I can never muster the proper enthusiasm to say, "Wow, hey great, that's just a super idea. God, you guys are brilliant." I mean, I can say the words, but when I don't *feel* them, it's painfully obvious.

After submitting character and background designs, we were awarded the job. We did it on time with no problem meeting the deadline, just me and Layron animating and Kyle Borth from Duck Soup handling the digital ink and paint and After Effects work. It came out great and everyone involved was happy with it.

Sadly, the agency ended up using a different composer.

But there are lessons in this story that reinforce many previous lessons. When someone says a job is too difficult to do, that's an opportunity for you to step up and say "I can do it." And, things don't always end up the way they originally look like they will. I thought "Win for Life" would be a composing job, but it turned out to be a directing job.

With the small budget and tight deadline, the spot *should* have been very difficult and aggravating. However, it was actually hassle-free and fun. The ad agency was very reasonable and likeable. The payment was a little late but we eventually got it, so no harm, no foul.

And we won a Telly Award for animation with it. Awesome!

CHAPTER 33

The Punisher

In March 2004, Marvel Films released a live-action version of *The Punisher*. Less than three weeks before it was due out, Duck Studios (Duck Soup had just changed its name) was asked to animate the opening titles for very little money and with an extremely short schedule (two weeks to do a minute and a half of animation).

Of course, Duck immediately asked Evil Cat Land if we were interested. It was another job for the kids who would eat bugs on a dare and we said yes. It was a tremendous amount of work to do in a short time, but it was also a high-profile project.

With so little time there was no room for error and, of course, there were *many* errors. And yet, somehow, we emerged victorious.

One of the reasons we had trouble was that the animation had to be extremely slow. EXTREMELY slow. If you have seen the *Punisher* titles, you know there is lots of slow-motion smoke and dripping blood. And if you understood the lessons in this book about 24 frames per second, you know that to make something move REEAALLLYY SLLLOOOWW, the increments of movement between drawings must be very, very small.

In this case, the increments were often smaller than the width of a pencil lead, meaning it was nearly impossible to do inbetweens. No matter how diligent the inbetween artists were, the animation sometimes got jumpy.

But that was just a minor problem compared to late one night when the animation scanners broke down. We had hundreds of drawings to scan by the next morning, and suddenly we were shut down. When there's no room for error, that's about the worst kind of error that can occur.

Steve Thenell, who was in charge of making sure everything computer-related at Duck worked and worked well, was not a guerrilla-type person. He always did things the right way, and it worked out well for him. Yet, in this case, he recognized that he needed a new set of rules to go by.

First off, he came in to the studio very late to help out (the problem happened after 11 p.m. [of course], but he came in nevertheless). After consulting the manuals and somehow finding tech support on the phone, he still had no answer.

So he took the scanners apart, sprayed WD-40 on some of the parts, and put them back together.

And it worked!

Sometimes the answer is very simple. And sometimes a non-guerrilla-type will play guerrilla-style because there is no other way to win.

Other than that, it was a normal job. The company that hired us didn't pay us on time (unfortunately, that's normal in this business—and this company was even more normal about paying than most companies), and, even though we animated the opening credits, our names didn't appear in *any* of the movie's credits. You can't get much more normal than that, can you?

CHAPTER 34

All Up in My Grill

All right, this is not a happy chapter. In fact, I don't even really want to write it. But I will because there are lessons in it, and that's what this book is all about.

Soon after *The Punisher*, we bid on a commercial job for Weber Grills. The agency wanted very simple, childish characters, not much more than stick figures.

Unfortunately, we didn't believe them. We thought that even though they were *saying* they wanted it simple, if we actually gave them stick figures they would say "Why should we hire you? You can't even draw."

That was a mistake. In their eyes, the characters we gave them were too well drawn. And subsequent submissions which met their criteria still did not please them.

What happened was, with our first designs, we set ourselves up in their minds as people who could not follow directions. So, even when we *did* deliver what they wanted, they had already decided we *couldn't*.

What we *should* have done the first time was deliver *exactly* what they asked for *alongside* better drawings, in case they really wanted nicer art. It was a stupid mistake on my part and it lost us a lucrative job.

Lesson: GIVE THE CLIENT WHAT THEY ASK FOR EVEN IF YOU DON'T BELIEVE THEM. GIVE THEM SOMETHING ELSE AS BACKUP IF YOU FEEL THE NEED, BUT NEVER DISOBEY!

CHAPTER 35

The Sun

The *Punisher* job happened in February 2004. In July of that year, we were in the midst of a little break from work when Layron found us an interesting project. A live-action company wanted to do an animated music video for a group on Warner Bros. records called the Sun. They wanted three and a half minutes of animation done in two weeks for $2,000.

Even I, who over the years took so many jobs no one else would touch, thought that was ridiculous. Way too much work, not enough time, and the money amounted to $500/week for Layron and myself, which was not anywhere near our rate and certainly insane for the hours we'd need to put in.

So we said we'd do it. Why? The concept was intriguing. They wanted animation in a punk-rock Scooby Doo style, which seemed both fun and easy. The song, "My Girlfriend's Best Friend," had a nice melody and a powerful performance by the band. The Sun was a major-label act, so the project would have at least some promotion when it was done. Plus, we had nothing else going on at the moment so we figured what the hell, let's go for it.

Before starting, we made a point of telling all the people in the production company that they were getting us for a bargain and that we didn't usually work for such a low rate or on such a tight schedule. They said they understood.

In order to finish, we had to use every shortcut we knew: backgrounds created in Photoshop, recycled animation, etc. And in the end, about half the video looked great. The other half, well, we don't put that on our reel.

The problem was the people producing the video. While they *said* they understood how much work animation involved, in reality, they *didn't* understand.

They made us put caricatures of about twenty Warner Bros. executives in the video (that was how they sold the idea to the label—the executives would appear as animated characters). Just doing that wasted valuable time that could have gone into making the video tighter.

The executives all submitted photos to us from which we created their caricatures. One woman's photo showed her wearing glasses. So we drew her wearing glasses. A couple of days later we found out she was very angry about this. She had called the producers and said, "Why does my character have glasses? I don't wear glasses." Apparently we were supposed to be able to tell from the picture of her wearing glasses that she didn't wear glasses. I could see she definitely had the kind of IQ that guaranteed her success as a music executive. God bless her wonderful, contact-wearing soul!

A week into the job, some help arrived in the form of an After Effects compositor provided by the production company. In one scene he added a motorcycle driving across the background. But he wasn't an animator, so while everything we did was on twos, he slid the motorcycle across the background on ones, and with no wheel movement. As a result, it looked like it was done by a five-year-old. It didn't fit in with the rest of the work and planted a very amateurish blemish on the scene.

The lesson here is: BE VERY CAREFUL WHEN YOU WORK WITH PEOPLE WHO DON'T UNDERSTAND ANIMATION. Don't even get me started on the problems caused by the fact that they didn't understand the difference between 24 frames per second and 30 frames per second. YES, that IS important!

After that project they wanted us to do a test for another video they were doing for Warner Bros. This one was going to be in the "Waking Life" style: rotoscoped via Photoshop and After Effects.

We told them we could do ten seconds for the money they were offering. They gave us twenty seconds of footage and said, "It's only ten seconds more." We explained that ten seconds meant 240 more drawings, but it made no impact on them. They just figured we were suckers who could be conned into anything. We stopped working with them shortly thereafter.

Lesson: WHEN YOU ACCEPT A JOB FOR BELOW YOUR RATE, THAT LOWER RATE BECOMES YOUR NEW RATE IN THE EYES OF THE PEOPLE WHO HIRED YOU. THEY WILL HAVE NO RESPECT FOR YOU. IT'S UNFORTUNATE BUT VERY TRUE. ACT LIKE A SUCKER AND YOU WILL GET TREATED LIKE ONE.

CHAPTER 36

Sun Tzu Paraphrased

There is a saying in Sun Tzu's *Art of War* that goes: "If you wait by the river long enough, you will see the body of your enemy float by."

Similarly, if you wait by the river long enough in Hollywood, you can get a meeting with whomever you want to. Pretty much.

That same year, 2004, I got two big meetings for big projects I was working on. And they happened because I had waited by the river long enough.

Meeting number one was for the "Night Owl" project. We had already pitched the idea at Comedy Central to a bunch of junior executives who only wanted to get Adam West's autograph, and it was a big waste of time. The leader of these junior idiots said she'd explain the idea to her bosses and get back to us. I knew then the answer would be no.

The agent who set up that meeting said the only other outlets we had were TV Land and Adult Swim. He said he had no contacts at Adult Swim but he would try and get us a meeting with TV Land. But, he added, it would be better if we changed the entire series and made it for kids because he had more contacts with kids networks.

He had no luck with the head of TV Land because, he said, the guy was an asshole. I accepted this for a month or so, but I really felt that the project was right for TV Land. So I decided that I must know someone who could set up a meeting with them.

I did some online research and found that the man in charge at TV Land, the "asshole," Sal Maniaci, had worked on a project with Stone

Stanley a couple of years before. So I asked Stone Stanley if they could provide an introduction for me.

David Stanley sent Sal a very nice, charming letter, describing me as funny and talented, and then, the very next day, nothing happened. But then, the week after that, nothing happened again.

Then one day, a few months later, as I sat by Sun Tzu's river, I got an e-mail from Sal's office saying he would be in town in two days, and could I meet with him? So I said yes, met with him, pitched the idea, and he passed on it because they were only doing reality shows for original programming at TV Land at the moment.

But it turned out he *wasn't* an asshole; he was just busy running a network and that's why he was hard to get a hold of. He was a very nice person, actually.

A month after that, I met with Russell Simmons about another project, again because of that whole sitting by the river thing. You remember Muffla and L.A. Posse and *Hip Hop Toonz* and how I met Muffla through my friend Cassandra who I met through my friend Dave who I met in New York working on a low budget feature seventeen years earlier, and how I got on that feature through a contact I made working on *Lemon Sky* at WGBH while still in college?

So, knowing Muffla can be traced back to a series of events that started in college. And Muffla, who had worked with Russell Simmons for years producing LL Cool J records, got me the meeting with the industry mogul.

I can't talk about the project because it's still brewing around top-secret style. But I can say Russell Simmons is a very cool guy who doesn't act like a powerful multimillionaire. He's just real.

So, wait by the river for your meeting. The river flowed for seventeen years before it brought Russell Simmons by. Of course, I didn't realize I was sitting by the river because I was busy with other things. But the river sometimes brings unexpected things many years after you first reach it.

CHAPTER 37

In Her Shoes

Near the end of summer 2004, while we were working on some smaller, fairly low-key projects, Mark Medernach told us we were being considered for a job doing animated titles for a live-action movie called *In Her Shoes.* The film's producer invited us to see a rough edit of the film that evening so we could get a feel for it.

So Layron and I went to the studio lot that evening to see the rough cut. Going onto studio lots always gives me a little rush because when I was a kid I thought the movie business was this wonderful, magical thing. When I'm on a lot, walking amongst the big stages, seeing the costume departments and the writers' buildings, I almost believe it again. Of course, the second I hear, "Excuse me, *sir*, are you supposed to be here?" the buzz is gone.

This movie was a big deal. It was produced by Ridley Scott (*Blade Runner*, etc.), directed by Curtis Hansen (*L.A. Confidential, Eight Mile*), and starred Cameron Diaz (*National Enquirer* forty-seven weeks per year).

At the screening, Cameron and Justin Timberlake sat a couple of rows in front of us. They were both very friendly and said hello a couple of times that evening, which I thought was very un-stuck-up of them. They seemed like cool, real people, although at the time I didn't know what Justin Timberlake looked like so I didn't know it was him hanging out with Cameron until someone told me later on.

I enjoyed the movie. I thought the story was interesting and well written. The acting was good, as was the directing. In short, I was happy to be working on the film; it had *quality*.

After the screening we met briefly with the director and producer to find out if they had any specific wants for the titles, and we spent the next couple of days coming up with designs.

Their only request was that the drawings be simple and childlike, which was a reasonable request. We pitched a few ideas to them later in the week and didn't hear back from them.

Then, two weeks later, they called and said we had the job. I had given up on the job by then, which, of course, I shouldn't have. One of the earliest lessons in this book is about how projects might not *really* be dead, even if they SEEM dead. Patience, while maybe not a virtue, is certainly not a bad thing.

During this time I was not only burning my candle at both ends and in the middle, but I had also borrowed another candle and was burning that as well, though merely at both ends. Under that self-indulgent metaphor lies this: in addition to working fourteen hours a day (or more) on *In Her Shoes*, I was running eleven miles a day, I was studying counterpoint and harmony at UCLA and I was getting my new band ready to play a concert at a United Nations celebration in Pasadena.

Luckily, for the most part, *In Her Shoes* was stress-free. Which meant there weren't too many last-minute changes from the client and we could concentrate on our work.

But there will always be *some* last-minute changes, and, no matter how seemingly small, in animation, that almost always mean lots more work.

The changes to this project were mainly things like, "Oh, the legal department said so-and-so's name needs to go before such-and-such's but has to be smaller than whatshername's." Or, "No, all those names can only be on for two seconds, not two and a half," which, while *sounding* innocuous, meant retiming everything.

And timing was important because the picture was cut to music, and when the animation hits on beats, it looks really cool. However, if you remember way back in the instructional part of this book, when I talk about music, I said that even if you put music onto a piece blindly, some things will hit perfectly just by chance.

That was a secret we relied on with this project, especially with all the timing changes. When the producer at Duck asked me what I was going to do about getting the beats to hit properly after the film's producers gave us a new, longer edit of the music to use, I told her not to worry and explained that we had a 90 percent chance of things hitting nicely without even trying. She gave me this look that was a cross between, "You're crazy" and "You're going to get me in trouble," but merely said, "Are you sure?"

After seeing the next cut, Carol Fenelon, the movie's producer, said, "By the way, you're doing a great job keeping the picture synched with the music." My theory was vindicated! (Just for the record, had the picture not automatically looked good with the new music, I would have spent whatever time was necessary to make it right. But I knew it wouldn't be necessary.)

Apart from some additional minor changes regarding the order of names, the project ended smoothly. Then, two days after we delivered the final cut, we got a call from Carol and Curtis saying that they had screened the film with the titles to some executives and that Ridley Scott said the animation was great but they weren't going to use it in the picture.

Things like that never surprise me; I've seen so many strange things go wrong on a project that *nothing* surprises me. After the screening, several people said that animated credits seemed too light-hearted for a film with such dark, heavy overtones as *In Her Shoes*. Me, I didn't agree, but I didn't say anything; I could tell by the finality in their voices that the decision was irrevocable. But it wasn't a big deal to me.

It's funny, when people give you news like that, they expect you to take it badly. I could tell Carol and Curtis expected us to be upset; they had a slight "walking on eggshells" tone in their voices. But we were fine with it.

True, it was disappointing not to be able to go to the local Cineplex and see our work on the big screen (though only a few months before we had gotten to see our *Punisher* titles). But we got paid, and we produced a very nice piece of film that we're proud of. So it was all good, as they say.

CHAPTER 38

The Collapse

We finished on schedule. We got paid on time. Just as the job was finishing, David Stanley called me to see if I could animate a logo for his new production company. He had just produced a show for Nick at Nite and wanted a five-second animated logo to place at the end.

I gave him some designs, which he liked, and on that Friday, which happened to be the last day of *In Her Shoes*, I agreed to animate the logo for him over the weekend.

Things were certainly looking good. One job done, another starting immediately. Layron was busy animating stuff for *The Nanny Reunion* on Lifetime, but another animator was available to help out. True, I had to cancel the United Nations concert, but other than that . . .

Well, actually, I wasn't feeling very well that day. Kind of nauseous and dizzy. And when I did my eleven-mile run, I still felt bad. And I hadn't finished my music homework yet and class was the next morning—so I would have to stay up all night doing it.

But by the time I got home, I felt so bad, I decided to go to bed early and get up at 5 a.m. to do my homework.

Around eleven that night I got up and walked over to the bathroom. I remember thinking, "I've never felt this bad in my life." I was dizzy, nauseous, and had a headache. So I started thinking to myself, "Okay, I won't go to class tomorrow. I'll e-mail the Professor and get the next assignment, then spend the next week leisurely catching up (since I'll have some time off from work after the logo is done.) Yes, that was a good plan. I started to feel better.

Then I heard my wife saying, "Oh my God, oh my God!" and I opened my eyes and saw her face swirling in front of me. Apparently I had never made it to the bathroom. I had collapsed and was on the floor twitching as I made these plans to skip class and do my homework the next week.

The lesson here: HARD WORK IS OKAY, BUT JESUS, DON'T KILL YOURSELF! AND ONLY A MORON RUNS ELEVEN MILES WHEN HE'S FEELING THAT SICK.

I slept until ten the next morning, then went to Duck to do the logo job. We got it done and I delivered it on Monday, but I felt very weak the whole time. In fact, I felt weak for the next few months. I had to cut back on my running and I was just very slow about everything. It took me quite a long time to recover from 2004.

CHAPTER 39

A Postscript

Six months after *In Her Shoes* finished, however, we were informed that the animation was going to be resurrected and included as a bonus feature for the DVD release. Great news indeed!

A week after that, I was told that the rights to the music used in the titles were too expensive, so the animation had been cut from the DVD as well. If I had only found out earlier, I would have written some music for *free* goddammit!

CHAPTER 40

If You Can't Bring the Mountain to Mohammed, You're a *Wuss*!

My absolute *least* favorite network in the history of television is Spike TV. As soon as it launched, I knew it was stupid. So when an agent I was working with a few years back told me that Spike TV was looking for animated content, I declined. But, he persisted, if I could rework some of my ideas and make the main characters strippers and hookers with giant breasts then there was a good chance I could possibly sell something to this wonderfully enlightened network. But I stood firm.

Therefore, when in late 2005 Layron said he'd found some possible work for us animating segments of an original Spike TV skit comedy show, my initial reaction was: "But Spike TV is shit."

However, this project was intriguing: we would create a fake 2D videogame, like *Street Fighter*, only featuring famous religious characters like Jesus and Mohammed. As a premise, it was actually funny, and creating a fake videogame would be interesting and engaging work.

There were several producers on the project, but the one we had the most contact with, Justin Roiland, was a nice guy and intelligent as well. I had expected some asshole in a Hustler t-shirt, reeking of Axe and making fart jokes, but Justin seemed to be a human being. We later met with other Spike producers who were typical type-A, ruthless, lying Hollywood-types, but our initial point of contact was decent.

After checking out some videogames for reference, Layron and I set about creating some sample art. Layron drew the characters and I built a computer game fighting world. In keeping with my guerrilla upbringing, I made a lot of it out of old artwork I kept on file, modifying it with Photoshop.

They liked our sample at Spike and we got the job. And, for a while, it was enjoyable work. We successfully created what looked like a real videogame (an obvious trick to this is using the mosaic filter in After Effects to give everything a bitmapped, slightly low-res, computer graphic look).

Despite the fact that Spike TV's executive geniuses had much input on the script, it was still *almost* funny. But the graphics were *tight*. We nailed it. Then we did a second installment.

When the show premiered, I forced myself to watch it. What can I say? How about, "Badly written, poorly conceived, horribly paced, with a needlessly smug attitude that made me wish I was dead"? But *our* part at least *looked* good, which meant I had made a long, strange journey in my career from films with funny, original content that looked like crap to pretty much the exact opposite.

A couple of weeks later, I got a phone call from some of the show's producers. They had an especially "We're-very-important-executives" tone in their voices that day.

They asked if I had posted any of the show's animation on the web. I said I hadn't. Did I know of any places it was posted? No, I didn't. Then one said, "I'm sure you know why we're asking this." I assured him I had no idea.

This was at the time that there was some protesting from the Islamic community over a European cartoon featuring Mohammed. There were some death threats, I believe, as well. So the big brains at Spike were panicking that someone would kill them because Mohammed was a character in the animation we did.

I said, "Oh, I never even thought of that. I doubt there will be a problem."

"You obviously haven't been watching the news," I was told. That was true. The only thing I watch less than the news is Spike TV. "This is serious," they said. "Our lives could be in danger."

A less hysterical producer chimed in. He was feeling even more important than the panicky guy. "I know there's the whole moral issue about freedom of speech, but I think we've got to pick our battles and this is one we should walk away from."

I politely refrained from saying, "But I'm sure nobody watches your stupid show, least of all Islamic fundamentalists. You're not important enough to be killed. Unfortunately."

What I did say, I think, was, "Whatever."

He reiterated. "We need to pick our battles and this is just not one of them."

"So we're pulling the segments from the show," another producer said.

"Why not just cut out the Mohammed parts?" I suggested. Apparently this was still too risky. You see, these Spike TV producers were now BOLD and IMPORTANT players on the world stage, DYNAMIC MEN deeply involved in one of history's most important moments. One little misstep could mean the END OF CIVILIZATION AS WE KNOW IT.

I was ordered to immediately destroy all computer files and original artwork from the segments—eliminate everything in case some Islamic terrorist broke into our studios, randomly went through the computers, and found a picture of Mohammed. I mean, it *could* happen, right?

I told them I'd take care of it right away. Now they could sleep easier, knowing they had helped mankind narrowly escape carnage and destruction on a scale never before conceived.

Of course, it was another week before I actually bothered to go into the studio and delete the files. I was busy with other things and this was *stupid*.

And guess what? None of the bold and important Spike TV executives were harmed in any way. Because nobody watched their stupid show anyway. *Stupiiid.* . . .

Spike TV. The network for REAL MEN.

CHAPTER 41

Passing It On

Here are a few last words of wisdom, starting with what I feel is the most important.

1. YOU ARE NOT A DIRECTOR UNTIL YOU FINISH A FILM!!!

   There are many people with good ideas who talk about them but never make them.

   And when I say "finish a film," I don't mean taping some drunken skit with your friends in your living room. I mean you make something that can get on television or into a film festival. Remember, people can't visualize your ideas—*you must show them*. Don't bore people with talk about your great idea for a series—MAKE IT!

2. If you really want to do something, then "No" cannot mean "No," it must merely mean that "Yes" is going to be difficult to achieve.

3. Try to avoid doing things you don't believe in, i.e., try not to sell out.

4. Don't feel too bad during those times when you are forced to sell out in order to pay the bills.

5. Enjoy life while doing as little harm as possible (unless it's *cool* harm).

Appendix

RECOMMENDED BOOKS

The Animator's Survival Kit by Richard Williams

If you decide you want to become a serious animator, move on to this amazing text filled with advanced, detailed examples of various animation techniques.

The *Human Figure in Motion* and *Animals in Motion* by Eadweard Muybridge

Both these books are great sources of reference as well as resources for cheating, containing frame by frame photographic breakdowns of various human and animal movements which you can examine (or steal).

The books tend to be expensive but you can find most of the photo sequences online. Just search for "Muybridge" plus whatever specific motion you are seeking (such as "cat walk"). Dover Books has published an edition with the photos on CD-Rom as well.

ANIMATION SOFTWARE

Thirty-day trial versions of Adobe Flash, After Effects, Photoshop, and Premiere can be downloaded from www.adobe.com.

Great Flash plug-ins, including one to give your characters moveable skeletons, can be tried and purchased at www.trickorscript.com.

DigiCel FlipBook is an awesome 2D program whose basic package is very affordable and excellent for pencil tests and creating animated layers for later use in After Effects. A free trial version is available at www.digicelinc.com.

Anime Studio Pro is a program that allows you to build and animate characters right in the software. A free trial version can be found at http://my.smithmicro.com/win/animepro/index.html.

ANIMATION SUPPLIES

Inexpensive animation paper (10 field student bond), peg bars (both Acme and their own brand, which will work with regular three-hole-punch paper), and just about anything else you'll need can be found at www.lightfootltd.com.

The original supply house for the Hollywood animation industry, Cartoon Colour, still sells cel paints and cels, along with paper, peg bars, etc., at www.cartooncolour.com.

Plexiglas can be purchased many places. Here's an inexpensive one: www.estreetplastics.com/White_Plexiglass_Sheets_s/84.htm

AUDIO SOFTWARE

High-end audio software can be very expensive, but here are some links where you can find free audio programs:

http://audacity.sourceforge.net

www.freedownloadscenter.com/Multimedia_and_Graphics/Misc__Sound_Tools/Sound_Recorder_Pro.html

If you want a reliable though kind of pricey program, Adobe Audition can be downloaded at www.adobe.com.

ORGANIZATIONS

Animation World Network has extensive job listings, links to schools, and many current articles about the industry. They can be found at www.awn.com.

Women in Animation is an excellent international organization: http://wia.animationblogspot.com.

The International Animated Film Society (ASIFA) can sometimes be beneficial to an animator. The international branch can be found here: http://asifa.net, and the Hollywood branch here: www.asifa-hollywood.org. There are local branches all over the world as well.

FLASH ADVICE

If you want to learn how to take your flash advice to the next level (and beyond), go to: www.coldhardflash.com.